Major U.S. Statistical Series

Definitions, Publications, Limitations

JEAN SLEMMONS STRATFORD
JURI STRATFORD

American Library Association
Chicago & London   1992

Cover design by David Niergarth
Text design by Mark Hoover and David Niergarth

Composed by Digital Graphics, Inc. in Berkeley Oldstyle using T$_E$X.
    Reproduction copy set on a Varityper 4300P phototypesetter

Printed on 55-pound Glatfelter, a pH-neutral stock, and bound in
10-point C1S cover stock by Edwards Brothers, Inc.

The paper used in this publication meets the minimum requirements of
American National Standard for Information Sciences—Permanence of Paper
for Printed Library Materials, ANSI Z39.48–1984. ⊗

Library of Congress Cataloging-in-Publication Data

Stratford, Jean Slemmons, 1955–
        Major U.S. statistical series : definitions, publications,
    limitations / Jean Slemmons Stratford, Juri Stratford.
            p.   cm.
        Includes index.
        ISBN 0-8389-0600-1
        1. United States—Statistical services 2. Social sciences—
    United States—Statistical methods. I. Stratford, Juri, 1955– .
    II. Title.
    HA37.U55S77   1992
    001.4'22'0973—dc20   92-16746

Printed in the United States of America.

96 95 94 93 92   5 4 3 2 1

To Ian

Contents

Figures and Tables

Acknowledgments

This book would not have been written without the support of a number of individuals. We would like to extend special thanks to the following people who provided support, encouragement, and comments: Herbert Bloom of American Library Association Publishing Services; Bill Katz and Joe Morehead, State University of New York, Albany; Steven M. Sheffrin, Department of Economics, University of California, Davis; and Steven D. Zink, University of Nevada, Reno.

Introduction

The United States government is perhaps the largest producer of statistical data in the world. Federal statistical programs gather data on a variety of topics, running the gamut from demography and economics to crime, education, health, and natural resources. Virtually every federal agency collects and disseminates data relevant to its spheres of influence. These data are intended to support the execution of agency mandates, the evaluation of national conditions, and the assessment and fine-tuning of public programs and policies. The data also may have numerous and varied secondary applications.

The purpose of this text is to provide readers with a framework for locating and understanding statistical data. The book describes the sources, construction, and publication of a number of basic statistical measures in several broad categories. These categories are population, labor force, U.S. economic indicators, price indexes and inflation, production, foreign trade, and U.S. federal government finance. This book provides an introduction to data producers, concepts, and publications in each of these subject areas, as well as the operating definitions and methodologies of major statistical measures. These measures have been selected to provide a representative sample of socio-economic statistics including several of the most important or frequently cited economic measures such as Gross National Product and the Consumer Price Index. The discussion illustrates the inherent limitations of the data series covered. This discussion is intended to support informed use of statistical data by providing information that will help readers locate and understand available measures. By examining a few key data series, this volume provides readers with an introduction that should be transferable to other categories of statistical data. The book is principally intended to assist and inform library and information professionals who deal with statistical measures in a reference setting. It may also be of use to a wide range of data users in business, government, and academic settings.

Basic Concepts

Statistical measures are the numeric representation of a variable (or characteristic) of a sample or population. In order to arrive at a numeric representation, data producers must make a number of decisions as to what to count, how the count will be made, and how the results of that count will be expressed. These decisions are governed to a great extent by the uses for which the data are intended. For example, before collecting employment statistics, the U.S. Bureau of Labor Statistics must decide whether to count unpaid work in family businesses, whether (and how) to survey, and at what levels of geography to produce data. Once made, these decisions will govern appropriate uses of the data by both the data producer and secondary users.

The choice of definitions for key terms or concepts is critical. There is no one *a priori* definition for most important statistical measures. For example, there is no one definition of "unemployment." In fact, the U.S. Bureau of Labor Statistics alone calculates eight different unemployment rates that vary in the breadth of their definition of key terms. The bureau then designates one of these eight rates as the official unemployment rate.

Frequently, statistics attempt to quantify some large-scale economic process or social characteristic. In such cases, comprehensive data generally cannot be gathered by direct observation. Again, using the example of unemployment data, it is not practical for the U.S. Bureau of Labor Statistics to gather data on total unemployment by direct observation—that is, by making a monthly count of all those persons in the United States who meet the bureau's various definitions of "unemployment." Instead, unemployment data are gathered by other means, including a sample survey (the Current Population Survey) and the reporting of new claims for state unemployment insurance benefits. The methodology employed in collecting and presenting statistical data has a critical impact on appropriate uses of the data.

Data users frequently have a hypothesis that they wish to test and need to locate appropriate datasets for that purpose. In such instances, users may be faced with two special problems. The first problem is to determine the range of available data. This task will be aided by knowledge of the programs and products of relevant data producers. The second problem is the evaluation of the relevance of each available data series to the inquiry at hand. A number of factors can come into play in this evaluation, among them data definitions employed and frequency of data collection, presentation, and publication. For example, a number of measures are available to track the related concepts of inflation and cost of living. There are statistics appropriate for analyzing the change in price levels over time for various categories of expenditure or segments of the population. There are also measures that facilitate geographic comparisons at a specific point in time.

Organization

The basic organization of this book is as follows. The first seven chapters are each devoted to a single major subject area: population statistics; labor force statistics; U.S. economic indicators; U.S. price indexes and inflation measures; gross national product (GNP) and other measures of production; foreign trade; and federal government finance. These chapters provide background on the activities of key data producers in the field under consideration, outline basic definitions for the range of measures available, describe the methodology behind the measures insofar as it contributes to an overall understanding of the general applicability and usefulness of the data, and list basic published sources of the data, as well as methodological and background sources. At the end of each chapter, a bibliography provides full references to works cited and consulted in the compilation of that chapter, including both data sources and methodological information.

The final chapter of the volume covers a number of basic concepts of data compilation and presentation. These concepts apply to a variety of statistical data series, including some of those covered in the first seven chapters of the book. Procedures and techniques covered in this section include estimated data and revision of estimates; sampling error; questionnaire design; indexing; methods of annual comparison; seasonal adjustment; current and constant dollar estimates; and variant data sources. The discussion includes examples from published data sources.

In the body of the text, discussion of data sources is limited to print materials. However, the authors recognize that, increasingly, users are interested in access to machine-readable forms of statistical data. In order to avoid needless duplication of information in the body of the work, the authors have provided information on the availability of machine-readable formats as an appendix.

Caveats and Limitations

Neither the selection of statistical measures nor the selection of bibliographic sources presented in this work can be considered comprehensive.

There are a number of indexes and bibliographies that provide comprehensive access to published statistics or methodological works. These include *American Statistics Index, Statistical Reference Index, Index to International Statistics, Statistics Sources,* and *Guide to Statistical Materials Produced by Governments and Associations in the United States.* Rather than duplicate the coverage provided in these works, the authors intended to describe only the data producer's own official sources of published data and important methodological works relevant to the analysis and understanding of the data series under discussion. Readers seeking more comprehensive access to published sources of data, as well as similar background information for data series not covered here, should consult the works mentioned above.

No one can gain an intimate mastery of the social and economic measures discussed here by perusing a single text. This volume deals neither with the science of statistics nor with the intentional or unintentional misuse of statistical data in the social science literature, but rather with such basic concepts as what is measured, and how and where that measure is presented. Other works dealing with the more technical problems of social statistics (e.g., *Misused Statistics* and *The Data Game*) may be consulted for information of that sort.

This text is not exhaustive. The discussion here is limited to a few key examples from which it is hoped that readers may gain a basic framework for locating, understanding, and evaluating data sources. Neither is this volume intended to serve as a reference that provides up-to-date information on statistical sources, methodology, and definitions. While every effort has been made to provide current, accurate information, by the time this work appears in print some of the specifics provided undoubtedly will be dated. (For example, the journal *Business Conditions Digest* ceased publication with the March 1990 issue. At that time, the Bureau of Economic Analysis announced that a scaled-down version of the information formerly presented there would now appear in the *Survey of Current Business.* In addition, the bureau indicated that adjustments in presentation might be forthcoming, and the treatment of former supplements and historic data was left unclear. Therefore, the present volume makes every effort to reflect the current status of coverage in *Survey of Current Business* and cites the supplements to *Business Conditions Digest* that formerly had been issued. But it was virtually impossible to provide complete information on the merging of information from *Business Conditions Digest* into *Survey of Current Business.* In addition, as this volume goes to press, the Bureau of Economic Analysis has announced a benchmark revision of its National Income and Product Accounts that includes a shift from the traditional measure of U.S. production, Gross National Product, to the more internationally comparable Gross Domestic Product. This shift is noted in chapter 5; however, the full ramifications of the change are not yet clear.) No statement in this work should be accepted as current fact—rather the work is intended to demonstrate principles and concepts that may be applied by data users to develop an understanding of statistical data. This knowledge should help readers locate and evaluate the current literature as needed.

It is the authors' hope that this work will serve as a prologue to informed use of social and economic statistics by data users and those assisting them in their search for information.

Bibliography

American Statistics Index. Bethesda, Md.: Congressional Information Service, monthly.

Index to International Statistics. Bethesda, Md.: Congressional Information Service, monthly.

Jaffe, A. J., and Herbert F. Spirer. *Misused Statistics: Straight Talk for Twisted Numbers*. New York: Marcel Dekker, 1987.

Maier, Mark H. *The Data Game: Controversies in Social Science Statistics*. Armonk, N.Y.: M. E. Sharpe, 1991.

Statistical Reference Index. Bethesda, Md.: Congressional Information Service, bimonthly.

Stratford, Juri, and Jean Slemmons Stratford. *Guide to Statistical Materials Produced by Governments and Associations in the United States*. Alexandria, Va.: Chadwyck-Healey, 1987.

Wasserman, Jacqueline O'Brien, and Steven R. Wasserman. *Statistics Sources*. 12th ed. Detroit, Mich.: Gale Research, 1989.

1   Population Statistics

Although the U.S. Census of Population and Housing is typically associated with collecting population statistics to determine the number of inhabitants, the census also provides a wide range of information on social and economic characteristics of the population, such as household composition, ethnicity, and income. Census data have a variety of applications. The decennial census is required by the U.S. Constitution to apportion seats in the House of Representatives, as well as for redistricting. Census data are used by public agencies at all levels of government for planning facilities and services that must be fine-tuned to population changes and movements. Population statistics are also fundamental to a broad range of research conducted by the private sector.

Several basic factors must be understood in order to use population data in an informed manner. First, it is necessary to understand the methodology under which the data were compiled. It is also critical to note the definitions employed in the publication of census data. While population characteristics are often described using vocabulary from common speech, these terms take on specialized meanings in the context of the census, and an understanding of these definitions is key for data users. In addition, due to the scale involved with large surveys and actual enumerations, imperfections of methodology should be noted because they may have a significant impact on the quality and applicability of the data. Finally, political bias and social bias are also important issues.

Census of Population and Housing

The U.S. Census of Population and Housing is conducted by the Bureau of the Census, which was established in 1902. The bureau is a general purpose statistical agency that collects, tabulates, and publishes statistical data. Its primary functions include the Constitutionally mandated decennial census of population and housing; quinquennial economic censuses of agriculture, government, manufactures, mineral industries, distributive trades, construction, and transportation; periodic surveys that provide information on many of the subjects covered in the censuses; U.S. foreign trade statistics on imports, exports, and shipping; and population estimates and projections.

A census is typically an enumeration. The United Nations lists four essential features of a population census: first, each individual is enumerated separately and the characteristics of that person are recorded separately; second, the census covers a precisely defined territory and includes every person present or residing within its scope; third, the population is enumerated with respect to a well-defined reference period; and fourth, censuses are taken at regular intervals.[1] While the U.S. decennial Census of Population and Housing satisfies the above definition, additional data on the population are gathered through sample surveys conducted as part of the decennial activities of the bureau.

The decennial census is collected using two questionnaires: a short form and a long form. The short form includes the questions asked of all households and fulfills the Constitutional mandate for a complete enumeration. The long form supplements the short form with additional questions used to collect housing, social, and economic data from only a sample of the total population. The long form used in the 1980 census included additional questions on twenty-six population subjects and on twenty housing subjects. In 1990, the long-form questionnaire included twenty-six additional population questions and nineteen questions on housing subjects. Data derived from the short form are sometimes referred to as one hundred percent, or complete count data while data from the long form are referred to as sample data.

A variable rate sample is used for the distribution of the long-form questionnaire. That is, the percentage of households receiving the long form varies according to the size of the governmental jurisdiction. In small governmental units, a higher proportion of housing units receives the long form than in larger governmental units. In 1980, the long form was distributed to 50 percent of households in governmental jurisdictions with populations of fewer than 2500. These areas accounted for one-tenth of the nation's population in the 1980 census. The long form was distributed to 17 percent, or one in six households, for the remainder of the country. In 1990, a similar sampling rate was applied.[2]

While an enumeration is generally associated with household interviews, the U.S. Census of Population has been conducted by mail in recent years. In 1970, 60 percent of the population received and returned their questionnaires through the mail. In 1980, that figure rose to 90 percent. The Census Bureau expanded its use of the mail system to avoid census takers' bias; to allow respondents to complete the form at their convenience; to reduce the possibility of housing units being missed or duplicated; and to ensure a proper, unbiased sample through better controlled distribution of the sample questionnaires. The bureau used two methods to assemble the address list. First, commercial address lists with about 41 million addresses were purchased. These lists generally included only addresses in city mail delivery portions of urbanized areas. Second, the Census Bureau conducted research and consulted with local governments to obtain address information and compiled its own list. In 1980, this list was composed of 34.5 million additional addresses.[3]

Census Reports

The 1990 census obtained information on a variety of population and housing topics. Subjects for which complete count data were collected included sex, race and Hispanic origin, age, and marital status (for population) and type of unit or units in structure, number of rooms in unit, tenure (owned or rented), value of home or monthly rent, vacancy status, and congregate housing (for housing). The following categories of sample data were also collected: social characteristics; education (enrollment and attainment); place of birth, citizenship, year of entry; ancestry or ethnic origin; language; migration; disability; veteran status; employment and unemployment; occupation, industry, class of worker; place of work, commuting to work, travel time; work experience and income in 1989 (for population); heating; source of water and method of sewage disposal; autos, light trucks, vans; kitchen facilities; year structure built; year moved in residence; number of bedrooms; farm residence; shelter costs including utilities; condominium status; plumbing facilities; and telephone (for housing).[4]

Data from the 1990 census and associated sample surveys will be tabulated and published in several different report series. These series will be similar in content and organization to the reports from the1980 census. The printed series are as follows: Census of Population and Housing, Census of Population, and Census of Housing.

Census of Population and Housing

The Census of Population and Housing (CPH) series will consist of five separate reports. These are listed in Table 1-1. Each report provides population and housing unit counts by varying levels of census geography. Series CPH-1 and CPH-2 contain one hundred percent data; CPH-3 and CPH-4 contain a mixture of one hundred percent data and sample data; and CPH-5 contains sample data only.

Table 1-1. 1990 Census of Population and Housing Reports

Series	Title
CPH-1	Summary Population and Housing Characteristics
CPH-2	Population and Housing Unit Counts
CPH-3	Population and Housing Characteristics for Census Tracts and Block Numbering Areas
CPH-4	Population and Housing Characteristics for Congressional Districts
CPH-5	Summary Social, Economic and Housing Characteristics

Source: U.S. Bureau of the Census, *1990 Census of Population and Housing: Tabulation and Publication Program* (Washington, D.C.: U.S. Government Printing Office, 1989), p. 12–14.

Table 1-2. 1990 Census of Population Reports

Series	Title
CP-1	General Population Characteristics
CP-1-1A	General Population Characteristics for American Indian and Alaska Native Areas
CP-1-1B	General Population Characteristics for Metropolitan Statistical Areas
CP-1-1C	General Population Characteristics for Urbanized Areas
CP-2	Social and Economic Characteristics
CP-2-1A	Social and Economic Characteristics for American Indian and Alaska Native Areas
CP-2-1B	Social and Economic Characteristics for Metropolitan Statistical Areas
CP-2-1C	Social and Economic Characteristics for Urbanized Areas
CP-3	Population Subject Reports

Source: U.S. Bureau of the Census, *1990 Census of Population and Housing: Tabulation and Publication Program* (Washington, D.C.: U.S. Government Printing Office, 1989), p. 12–14.

Census of Population

The 1990 Census of Population (CP) materials will consist of nine different report series. These are listed in Table 1-2. The CP-1 series reports provide general population characteristics for various geographic areas. Data to be produced include age, sex, race, Hispanic origin, marital status, and household characteristics. Data in the CP-1 series reports are one hundred percent data. CP-2 series reports will focus on social and economic data gathered through the sample survey. CP-3 will provide approximately thirty special subject reports on topics ranging from migration to the older population. CP-3 series reports are based on sample data.

Census of Housing

The Census of Housing (CH) will include nine reports on housing topics. These are given in Table 1-3. The four-report series on general housing

Table 1-3. 1990 Census of Housing Reports

Series	Title
CH-1	General Housing Characteristics
CH-1-1A	General Housing Characteristics for American Indian and Alaska Native Areas
CH-1-1B	General Housing Characteristics for Metropolitan Statistical Areas
CH-1-1C	General Housing Characteristics for Urbanized Areas
CH-2	Detailed Housing Characteristics
CH-2-1A	Detailed Housing Characteristics for American Indian and Alaska Native Areas
CH-2-1B	Detailed Housing Characteristics for Metropolitan Statistical Areas
CH-2-1C	Detailed Housing Characteristics for Urbanized Areas
CH-3	Housing Subject Reports

Source: U.S. Bureau of the Census, *1990 Census of Population and Housing: Tabulation and Publication Program* (Washington, D.C.: U.S. Government Printing Office, 1989), p. 12–14.

characteristics CH-1 will provide statistics on housing units, such as units in structure, value and rent, number of rooms, and tenure and vacancies. These reports will be based on complete count data. The CH-2 reports will present detailed housing characteristics based on the 1990 sample survey. The housing subject report series CH-3 will include approximately ten reports on topics such as structural characteristics and space utilization drawn from the sample data.[5]

Additional Sources

There are several sources that provide background information on demographic data. The Census Bureau itself publishes many such aids. Among the most useful are *Census of Population and Housing: Users' Guide* and *Census '80: Continuing the Factfinder Tradition.* Both of these publications describe the Census of Population and Housing Program products, concepts, definitions, data limitations, geography, and so on. The Census Bureau's *Catalog* also provides a wealth of information on the products of the bureau, including printed and machine-readable data files. For information on the 1990 census, the bureau has produced *1990 Census of Population and Housing: Tabulation and Publication Program.* This monograph outlines the proposed content of the 1990 census questionnaire, census procedures, and information dissemination programs. The Census Bureau publication *The Methods and Materials of Demography*, by Shyrock and Siegel, provides basic background on demographic concepts, history, and methodology.

Current Population Survey

Estimates and projections are used to supplement census figures between enumerations. The primary source of data for these estimates and projections is the Current Population Survey (CPS). The CPS is conducted each month under the sponsorship of the U.S. Bureau of Labor Statistics (BLS) and is designed primarily to provide accurate national-level data on employment and unemployment. (The labor force data gathered from the CPS and published by BLS are the focus of chapter 2.) In addition, a wealth of demographic data obtained from the CPS sample is published by the Census Bureau in its own report series. These survey activities differ from the decennial census in two major respects. First, they are not designed to canvass an entire population—only a sample. Second, although participation in the decennial census is mandatory, response to the surveys is voluntary.

Population estimates may be produced in a variety of ways, including consulting population registers (such as voter registration rolls or military service records) or conducting sample surveys. Estimates also may be created by carrying forward the population from the last census either by employing mathematical extrapolation of past trends or by employing direct measurements of change: data reflecting birth, death, and migration. For example, the first population projections produced by the Census Bureau published in the 1850 and 1860 censuses were based on extrapolation of past trends. However, the methodology currently used by the Census Bureau was developed by Pascal K. Whelpton at the Scripps Foundation during the 1930s. Whelpton's projections used separate assumptions concerning fertility, mortality, and immigration. The Census Bureau adopted Whelpton's methods when he joined the bureau after the Second World War. Population projections are essentially estimates made for future dates. Both estimates and projections may be made by age, sex, marital status, and so forth, as well as for the total population. Moreover, estimates and projections are made for other demographic categories—marriages, households, the labor force, school enrollment, and so on.[6]

The *Current Population Reports* Series

At present, the demographic results of the Current Population Survey are published by the Census Bureau in eight report series: *Population Characteristics (P-20); Special Studies (P-23); Population Estimates and Projections (P-25); Local Population Estimates (P-26); Special Censuses (P-28); Consumer Income (P-60); Household Economic Studies*

(P-70); and *International Population* (P-95). These series are described briefly below.

Population Characteristics (P-20)

The annual reports in this series contain data on geographic residence and mobility, fertility, school enrollment, educational attainment, marital status, households and families, persons of Spanish origin, and various other topics. Biennial reports present information on voter registration and participation. This series absorbed the information on the size and characteristics of the farm population formerly published in *Farm Population* (P-27).

Special Studies (P-23)

This series provides information pertaining to methods, concepts, and specialized data. Included here are occasional reports on the black population, the metropolitan and nonmetropolitan populations, youth, women, and the older population.

Population Estimates and Projections (P-25)

This series presents monthly estimates of the total population of the United States by age, sex, and geographic area, as well as population projections. Also included are data on the components of population change. Prior to 1984, this series included information on local area population and per capita income. Beginning in 1984, this information was released as part of the P-26 series.

Local Population Estimates (P-26)

These reports provide population estimates for counties and metropolitan areas, using consistent methodology for those localities in every state. Also included, beginning in 1984, are population and per capita income estimates for local government jurisdictions. Previously, these estimates were released in the P-25 series.

Special Censuses (P-28)

These reports summarize the results of population censuses taken at the request and expense of city or other local governments.

Consumer Income (P-60)

Information concerning families, individuals, and households at various income levels is presented in this report series. Data are also presented on noncash benefits and the relationship of income to age, sex, race, family size, education, occupation, work experience, and other characteristics.

Household Economic Studies (P-70)

Approximately three reports per year are published in this series. Topics covered include educational background and economic status, pensions, layoff and job searches, and family support networks and assistance programs. Reports are generally compiled using longitudinal data from the Census Bureau's Survey of Income and Program Participation (SIPP), rather than from the CPS. The SIPP survey is a panel survey that has been conducted since 1984. Data from SIPP serve to supplement the census and the CPS.

International Population Reports (P-95)

This continuing series of reports presents estimates of demographic and economic data for selected Communist countries. Reports are prepared by the Foreign Demographic Analysis Division of the Census Bureau. Data are generally from official foreign government sources.

Census Terminology

An understanding of census terminology is crucial to the informed use of census data. Two types of terminology are important in this regard. The first is the vocabulary used to describe census concepts. The second is the terminology employed to describe census geography.

Frequently, census data are described using terms from common speech with commonly accepted meanings. However, in the context of the census, these terms take on very precise meanings that may differ from their commonly accepted meanings. For example, the term *family* is part of everyday speech. This term may refer to a person and all of his or her relatives; to parents and their children; or to all persons living in the same house. However, for the purposes of the decennial census, the Census Bureau uses the term *family* to mean "all persons who occupy a single housing unit and are related to the householder, usually the person in whose name the home is owned or rented." Thus, in census terminology, a family excludes any relatives not living in the same household (e.g., a son or daughter away at college) and other persons living in the housing unit who are not related to the householder (e.g., foster children or the live-in children of an adult who is not the householder and who is unrelated to the householder). In addition, persons living alone are not counted as families. They are, however, classified as households. The Census Bureau defines a household as the person or persons occupying a housing unit. In many instances, a household and a family will be the same; however, as noted above, where persons live alone, or with an unrelated householder, the term *family* will not apply.[7]

Geographic terms also play a crucial role when interpreting the published results of the census for states, counties, cities, and smaller areas. There are generally two types of geographic areas for which the Census Bureau tabulates data. The first type of census geography is administrative areas. The Census Bureau is not responsible for establishing the boundaries of the administrative areas for which it tabulates data. The legally established boundaries for areas such as states, counties, and cities are established by other authorities.

A second category of geographic areas is statistical areas. Some statistical areas are defined by the Census Bureau in conjunction with local advice. These areas include such divisions as blocks, block groups, tracts, and divisions. A block is the smallest level of census geography. Blocks may be as small as a normal city block or as large as several square miles. An average block in an urban area has a population of eighty-five persons. In a rural area, a block averages thirty persons. Blocks are grouped to build units of approximately one thousand persons. These units are known as block groups. Block groups, in turn, are nested in census tracts, having a population of approximately four thousand persons. Tracts are grouped within census county divisions (CCDs), formerly known as minor civil divisions. CCDs are, in turn, nested in counties.[8]

There are other statistical areas for which census data are tabulated that are defined by federal agencies other than the Census Bureau. Metropolitan statistical areas (MSAs), formerly known as standard metropolitan statistical areas (SMSAs), are defined by the Office of Management and Budget (OMB). MSAs are highly populated, economically integrated areas that meet one of the following criteria: (1) they contain a city of at least fifty thousand people or (2) they contain an urbanized area of at least fifty thousand and a total population of at least one hundred thousand (seventy-five thousand in New England). Urbanized areas consist of a central city or cities and surrounding closely settled territory, or an urban fringe, that together have a minimum population of fifty thousand.[9] The Census Bureau also reports data by zip code areas that are defined by the U.S. Postal Service.

Two fundamentally different principles are used to develop statistical areas. One principle calls for the definition of a statistical area on the basis of the similarity of its component parts. This is known as the homogeneity principle. Statistical areas delineated on the homogeneity principle are particularly useful for analyzing trends as well as differences between areas. Examples of such areas include Census Bureau tabulation of special purpose district data for the economic censuses (e.g., water-use regions, fishing regions, lumber industry regions, and oil and gas districts). The other principle employed in delineating statistical areas involves definition on the basis of a nucleus and an area of influence. This is known as the functional integration principle (e.g., a central city and its commuter suburbs). Functional areas include metropolitan areas, community and neighborhood areas, tribal areas, traffic flow areas, and all other areas that are integrated through communication or movement of one kind or another.[10]

Data Limitations

Census data (like other types of statistics) are subject to two broad categories of error: sampling error and nonsampling error. Sampling error is a specific measure of the error associated with the fact that only a portion of the entire population under consideration was surveyed. Nonsampling error accounts for a broad range of other possible data imperfections.

Sampling Error

Data derived from sample surveys are only estimates of what a complete count would have shown. Sampling error is a measure of variability that shows the range within which the true answer is likely to lie if the entire population could be counted. Most publications based upon sample data, including Census publications, provide information on calculating sampling error in the technical documentation. Specific examples of these calculations are provided in chapter 8.

Nonsampling Error

An enumeration is an accounting procedure rather than a statistical procedure. A correct enumeration is one for which all questionnaires are properly distributed, returned, and tabulated. An enumeration may be subject to a variety of procedural or nonsampling errors. Critics of enumeration cite two types of coverage errors: erroneous inclusions and omissions.[11]

Erroneous inclusions are: fictitious counts fabricated by enumerators, counted people who were born after or died before the census day, or multiple counts of the same individual. Because enumerators are paid more to enumerate occupied than vacant housing, they sometimes curbstone—that is, they list fictitious people as living at addresses without contacting anyone living inside the building or even determining whether the building is occupied or vacant. Also, families maintaining two residences may be mistakenly counted twice in the census.[12]

Omissions are people left out of the census who should have been counted. When errors of omission occur, the enumeration is subject to undercount. An undercount is the error that results from the failure to count some persons or housing units in the census. Some common reasons for omissions include households omitted from the Census Bureau's address list, households incorrectly enumerated as vacant, and individuals omitted when others in the household were counted. Other factors that influence the level of omissions, or undercount, include the number of homeless persons and migrant workers.

Undercounts are determined by comparing data from the enumeration to other estimates of the population. The Census Bureau conducts a Post-Enumeration Survey (PES) to provide an independent estimate of the population to aid in determining the completeness of the census. The PES essentially recanvasses selected small areas throughout the country shortly after the census has been taken. The results of the PES are then compared to the census results, and the Census Bureau assumes that the difference between the PES results and the census count is the same as the difference between the actual total population and the census results. This means that if the PES sample is smaller than the census count, the bureau assumes that there has been an overcount. If the PES sample is larger than the census count, undercount is assumed. While an overcount is hypothetically possible and does happen for some segments of the population, it is generally true that the PES estimates are larger than the actual enumeration, and the census is assumed to have undercounted the population.[13]

The Census Bureau recognizes that some statistical techniques may have the potential to provide more accurate data than an actual enumeration, and representatives of the bureau have argued that"it is the accuracy of this determination and not the method which is of primary constitutional significance." However, for the purposes of the 1980 census, the bureau also indicated that it would be impossible to apply these techniques to all levels of geography in an unbiased manner. In a prepared statement submitted before the Senate Subcommittee on Energy, Nuclear Proliferation and Federal Services, Vincent P. Barabba, then the director of the Census Bureau, indicated that "none of the currently known procedures [for adjustment] have been tested for their capability to measure undercount for all units of government" and therefore were not being used in the census.[14] In 1990, legal challenges to this position were successfully put forward, and a court decision in New York State required the Secretary of Commerce to consider adjusting for undercount. On July 15, 1991, the secretary announced that no such adjustment would be made; however, the legal debate is likely to continue as groups who believe that they would benefit by adjustment file lawsuits to force the issue.[15]

Under- or overcount is usually attributed to errors of omission like those listed above; however, tabulation errors may also be attributed to social and political bias. Based on his experiences on behalf of the World Health Organization (WHO) in East Pakistan, John Ratcliffe notes the inaccuracy of Near Eastern census data due to the fact that "neither Bangladesh, India, nor Pakistan corrects census data for underenumeration." This underenumeration is due, in part, to the fact that it is custom among the poor of some Near Eastern areas not to consider children younger than age five to be full-fledged family members and, therefore, not to report them to census takers. The governments do not make any attempt to correct their figures to account for this practice. Not only is this problem in the statistics uncorrected, but it is not mentioned in such widely held and respected sources as the United Nations' *Demographic Yearbook* and *Statistical Yearbook*.[16]

Enumerations may also be subject to other types of nonsampling errors, such as design and coding errors. In the 1970 census, the Census Bureau discovered that a substantial number of respondents erroneously indicated their decade of birth as the 1860s rather than the 1960s. The bureau determined that this was due to the fact that the box on the questionnaire for the 1860s came before the box for the 1960s. In another example of coding error from the 1970 census, a number of women in Philadelphia indicated their occupation as taxi dancer, a slang expression for prostitute. This was originally misinterpreted by census staff as taxi driver.[17]

Suppression of Data

Statistical agencies frequently guarantee respondents that the information they provide will be held in confidence. In the case of the census, confidentiality is also guaranteed by law. It is sometimes necessary to withhold or suppress information in order to honor that promise of confidentiality. This is especially true for data on the characteristics of very small groups, or at very small levels of geography, such as blocks or tracts. The suppression of data affects data users, particularly when they are aggregating data for groups of blocks or tracts.

The Census Bureau never suppresses certain basic counts for the Census of Population and Housing, even if an area has a count of only one. Other data elements may be suppressed, as necessary, primarily when the size of the population being characterized falls below a specified threshold. For the 1980 census, the bureau omitted data where suppression was necessary. In 1990, the bureau moved to a technique called *data switching* in cases where confidentiality was at stake. This technique involves switching data for one area with data from another area of similar size. Data switching will be invisible to data users and is preferable to suppression because data will be reported for areas that would have required suppression under the 1980 procedures.

Table 1-4. Characteristics of Housing Units, by Blocks: 1980—Bonneville County, Idaho

			Occupied Housing Units			
	Owner			Renter		
Blocks within Census Tracts or Block Numbering Areas (BNAs)	Total	Mean value (dollars), specified owner	Total	1.01 or more persons per room	Lacking complete plumbing for exclusive use	Mean contract rent (dollars), specified renter
Idaho Falls:						
210	8	35,900	5	2	—	199
211	20	51,000	19	—	—	235
212	55	56,700	1	. . .	. . .	. . .
213	30	41,400	4	. . .	. . .	. . .
214	32	43,000	4	. . .	. . .	. . .
215	24	41,200	3	. . .	. . .	. . .
216	15	45,000	1	. . .	. . .	. . .
217	62	59,700	4	. . .	. . .	. . .
218	19	69,700	—	—	—	—
219	26	75,500	1	. . .	. . .	. . .

Source: U.S. Bureau of the Census, *1980 Census of Population and Housing: Users' Guide* (Washington, D.C.: U.S. Government Printing Office, 1982), p. 104.

. . . not applicable; data withheld to avoid disclosure of information for individuals

— zero, or less than 0.1%

1980 Data Suppression Techniques

In 1980, the Census Bureau withheld, or suppressed, tabulations of characteristics of very small groups of people or very small geographic areas in order to maintain the confidentiality promised to respondents and required by law. The Census Bureau did not suppress total population, total housing units, year-round housing units, occupied units, vacant year-round housing units, and counts of persons and households in each race and Spanish-origin category. However, to protect confidentiality, complete counts of other characteristics such as age, race, or relationship were shown only if there were fifteen or more persons in the geographic area. This fifteen-person criterion applied only to the total, not to the characteristic in question. That is, characteristics such as age and race were reported only when the total count of persons exceeded fifteen, not the number of blacks or persons older than sixty-five. These rules would not prevent showing that there were two persons older than sixty-five as long as the total for the area was fifteen or more persons. The threshold for family, household, and housing unit data was five. The suppression of data may result in problems when trying to aggregate data for groups of small geographic areas such as blocks or tracts in any of the 1980 census report series based on complete count data. Table 1-4 provides block-level data from the 1980 census for Bonneville County, Idaho, and demonstrates the suppression of data. Data were reported for all owner-occupied units and all units in block numbering areas (BNAs) 210 and 211, but suppressed in BNAs 212 through 219, where the total number of units was fewer than five.

Notes

1. Henry S. Shyrock, Jacob S. Siegel, and Associates, *The Methods and Materials of Demography*, 4th ed. (Washington, D.C.: U.S. Government Printing Office, 1980), p.5.
2. U.S. Bureau of the Census, *1980 Census of Population and Housing: Users' Guide*; and U.S. Bureau of the Census, *1990 Census of Population and Housing: Tabulation and Publication Program* (Washington, D.C.: U.S. Government Printing Office), p.41 and p.3, respectively.
3. U.S. Bureau of the Census, *1980 Census of Population and Housing: Users' Guide*; and Eugene P. Erickson and Joseph B. Kadane, "Appendix 1: Estimating the Population in a Census Year: 1980 and Beyond," in *Federal Statistics and National Needs*, U.S. Senate, Committee on Governmental Affairs (98th Congress, 1st Session, Committee Print) (Washington, D.C.: U.S. Government Printing Office, 1984), p.41–45 and p.234–41, respectively.
4. Marshall L. Turner, Jr., "The 1990 Census and Its Data Products," *ICPSR Bulletin*, May 1991, p.1–5.
5. U.S. Bureau of the Census, *1990 Census of Population and Housing: Tabulation and Publication Program*, p.39–42.
6. Shyrock and Siegel, p.39–42.
7. U.S. Bureau of the Census, *Census '80: Continuing the Factfinder Tradition* (Washington, D.C.: U.S. Government Printing Office, 1980), p.161–63.
8. "Keys to Census Geography," *California State Census Data Center Newsletter*, January 1991, p.14.
9. U.S. Bureau of the Census, *1980 Census of Population and Housing: Users' Guide*, p.51.
10. U.S. Bureau of the Census, *Census '80: Continuing the Factfinder Tradition*, p.129–32.
11. Erickson and Kadane, "Appendix 1," p.234.
12. U.S. Congress, Senate, Committee on Governmental Affairs, *Undercount and the 1980 Census: Hearing, November 18, 1980* (Washington, D.C.: U.S. Government Printing Office, 1980), p.45.
13. Ibid., p.237; and "Post-Enumeration Survey," *California State Census Data Center Newsletter*, October 1990, p.6–7.
14. U.S. Congress, Senate, Committee on Governmental Affairs, *The Decennial Census: An Analysis and Review* (96th Congress, 2nd Session, Committee Print) (Washington, D.C.: U.S. Government Printing Office, 1980), p.73.
15. "The Census Won't Be Adjusted," *California State Census Data Center Newsletter*, August 1991, p.2.
16. John W. Ratcliffe, "International Statistics: Pitfalls and Problems," *Reference Services Review*, Fall 1982, p.94.
17. Erickson and Kadane, "Appendix 1," p.238–40; and U.S. Bureau of the Census, *Census '80: Continuing the Factfinder Tradition*, p.182–84.

Bibliography

Bean, Frank D., and Rodolfo O. de la Garza. "Illegal Aliens and Census Counts." *Society* (March/April 1988), p.48–53.

Jaffe, A. J., and Herbert F. Spirer. *Misused Statistics: Straight Talk for Twisted Numbers*. New York: Marcel Dekker, 1980.

Meyers, Ramon H. "Government Statistics in China." *Reference Services Review* (Fall 1982), p.93.

Ratcliffe, John W. "International Statistics: Pitfalls and Problems." *Reference Services Review* (Fall 1982), p.94.

Shyrock, Henry S., Jacob S. Siegel, and Associates. *The Methods and Materials of Demography*. 4th ed. Washington, D.C.: U.S. Government Printing Office, 1980.

Turner, Marshall L., Jr. "The 1990 Census and Its Data Products." *ICPSR Bulletin* (May 1991), p.1–5.

United Nations. *Demographic Yearbook*. New York: United Nations, annual.

United Nations. *Statistical Yearbook*. New York: United Nations, annual.

U.S. Bureau of the Census. *Census Catalog and Guide*. Washington, D.C.: U.S. Government Printing Office, annual.

――――. *Census '80: Continuing the Factfinder Tradition*. Washington, D.C.: U.S. Government Printing Office, 1980.

――――. *Counting for Representation: The Census and the Constitution*. Washington, D.C.: U.S. Government Printing Office, 1989.

――――. *Current Population Reports: Series P-20 Population Characteristics*. Washington, D.C.: U.S. Government Printing Office, irregular.

――――. *Current Population Reports: Series P-23 Special Studies*. Washington, D.C.: U.S. Government Printing Office, irregular.

――――. *Current Population Reports: Series P-25 Population Estimates and Projections*. Washington, D.C.: U.S. Government Printing Office, irregular.

――――. *Current Population Reports: Series P-26 Local Population Estimates*. Washington, D.C.: U.S. Government Printing Office, irregular.

――――. *Current Population Reports: Series P-27 Farm Population*. Washington, D.C.: U.S. Government Printing Office, irregular—absorbed by series P-20.

――――. *Current Population Reports: Series P-28 Special Censuses*. Washington, D.C.: U.S. Government Printing Office, irregular.

――――. *Current Population Reports: Series P-60 Consumer Income*. Washington, D.C.: U.S. Government Printing Office, irregular.

――――. *Current Population Reports: Series P-70 Household Economic Studies*. Washington, D.C.: U.S. Government Printing Office, irregular.

――――. *Current Population Reports: Series P-95 International Population Reports*. Washington, D.C.: U.S. Government Printing Office, irregular.

――――. "Evaluating of Population Estimating Procedures for Counties, 1980: An Interim Report." *Current Population Reports: Series P-25*. No. 984. Washington, D.C.: U.S. Government Printing Office, September 1986.

――――. "Evaluating of Population Estimating Procedures for States, 1980: An Interim Report." *Current Population Reports: Series P-25*. No. 933. Washington, D.C.: U.S. Government Printing Office, June 1983.

――――. *Factfinder for the Nation*. Washington, D.C.: U.S. Government Printing Office, irregular.

———. *1980 Census of Population and Housing: Users' Guide*. Washington, D.C.: U.S. Government Printing Office, 1982.

———. *1990 Census of Population and Housing: Tabulation and Publication Program*. Washington, D.C.: U.S. Government Printing Office, July 1989.

———. *Reflections of America: Commemorating the Statistical Abstract Centennial*. Washington, D.C.: U.S. Government Printing Office, 1980.

U.S. Congress. House. Committee of Post Office and Civil Service. Subcommittee on Census and Population. *Census Undercount and Feasibility of Adjusting Census Figure: Hearing, August 17, 1987*. Washington, D.C.: U.S. Government Printing Office, 1988.

———. *The Decennial Census Improvement Act: Hearing, March 3, 1988*. Washington, D.C.: U.S. Government Printing Office, 1988.

———. *Improving Census Accuracy*. 100th Congress, 1st Session, Committee Print. Washington, D.C.: U.S. Government Printing Office, 1987.

———. *Problem of Undercount in 1990 Census: Hearing, July 14, 1987*. Washington, D.C.: U.S. Government Printing Office, 1987.

———. *Proposed Guidelines for Statistical Adjustment of the 1990 Census: Hearing, January 30, 1990*. Washington, D.C.: U.S. Government Printing Office, 1987.

U.S. Congress. Senate. Committee on Governmental Affairs. *The Decennial Census: An Analysis and Review*. 96th Congress, 2nd Session, Committee Print. Washington, D.C.: U.S. Government Printing Office, 1980.

———. *Federal Statistics and National Needs*. 98th Congress, 1st Session, Committee Print. Washington, D.C.: U.S. Government Printing Office, 1984.

———. *Undercount and the 1980 Census: Hearing, November 18, 1980*. Washington, D.C.: U.S. Government Printing Office, 1980.

2   Labor Force Statistics

Labor force statistics are used by both the government and the private sector to gauge the supply of, demand for, and condition of labor in the United States. Labor force statistics provide information about the number and demographic characteristics of employed and unemployed persons and about the available labor pool. There is no one comprehensive federal program collecting detailed data on employment. The major source of federal labor force statistics is the U.S. Bureau of Labor Statistics (BLS). In addition to the BLS, the Census Bureau and the U.S. Department of Agriculture compile data on the labor force.

Various labor force surveys are conducted as part of programs across these three agencies. However, there is not one consistent or comparable system of methodologies and definitions that is common to all of the programs. Instead, each program employs its own methodology and operating definitions, which differ in varying degrees from one another.

U.S. Bureau of Labor Statistics

The conceptual framework and techniques employed to measure the U.S. labor force were developed in the 1930s by the Works Projects Administration (WPA). In 1942, responsibility for the data was transferred to the Census Bureau. Since 1959, BLS has had broad responsibility for the field of labor economics. Along with the Census Bureau, the BLS is one of the principal data-gathering agencies of the federal government. The BLS is responsible for the concept, analysis, and publication of data relating to employment, unemployment, and other characteristics of the labor force; prices and family expenditures; wages and other worker compensation, and industrial relations; productivity and technological change; and occupational safety and health.

The primary source of longitudinal data on the labor force is the Current Population Survey (CPS). While the CPS operation is conducted by the Bureau of the Census, and demographic data from the CPS are published by the bureau in its *Current Population Reports* (as described in chapter 1), the responsibility for the concept and analysis of the CPS rests with the BLS, which publishes labor force data based on the CPS in its own publication series. The CPS is designed to produce accurate data at the national level. In addition, the CPS provides accurate data for several states and local areas. The BLS also conducts the Local Area Unemployment Statistics (LAUS) program and the Current Employment Statistics program (CES), which supplement the CPS's coverage for less densely populated states and local areas.

BLS Labor Force Data

The Current Population Survey

The CPS provides data on the work status of the population. It is a survey of approximately sixty thousand households, conducted monthly in the week containing the twelfth day of the month. The sample is designed to provide accurate national-level data. In addition, the sample size and composition of the CPS are sufficient to produce accurate data for eleven highly populated states and two metropolitan areas.

Each month, on the basis of responses to survey questions, members of households in the CPS sample sixteen years of age and older are classified as "employed," "unemployed," or "not in the labor force." To be considered as "employed" during the survey week, a person must meet one of four separate criteria. The respondent must (1) have worked for one hour or more as a paid civilian, *or* (2) have worked at least fifteen hours in a family business without pay, *or* (3) be a member of the armed forces, *or* (4) be on an unpaid leave due to illness, bad weather, disputes between management and labor, or personal reasons. To be classified as "unemployed," a survey respondent must meet *all* of three separate criteria. He or she must have (1) had no employment in the past four weeks, *and* (2) been available to work at that time, *and* (3) have made specific effort to find work during that period. [1]

"Labor force" is defined as the total of employed and unemployed persons (per the definitions given above). Persons sixteen years of age and older who are not in the above categories are defined as "not in the labor force." This category generally is made up of housewives, students, retired persons, seasonal workers surveyed during an off season who were not actively looking for work, inmates, disabled persons, and discouraged workers.[2] "Discouraged workers" is defined by the BLS as those persons who (1) want to work, *and* (2) have not looked for work in the four weeks prior to the survey, *and* (3) have stopped looking for work because they do not believe that there are jobs available to them.[3] In addition, respondents are classed as "full-" or "part-time workers." Part-time workers work between one and thirty-five hours per week. Workers also can be classed as "part-time for economic reasons." Those persons who work part-time, but want full-time work and cannot find it, fall into this category.[4]

Unemployment Rates

There are eight different unemployment rates calculated by the BLS from CPS data. These rates, given in Table 2-1, are published in the monthly BLS news release "The Employment Situation." The rates vary by the breadth of their definitions of both "unemployment" and "labor force." Rates U-1, U-2, U-3, U-4, and U-5b include only the civilian labor force. The U-5a rate also includes resident armed forces. Rate U-6 makes some adjustment to count part-time workers for economic reasons as only partially employed. Rate U-7 does likewise and also makes adjustment for discouraged workers. Of these, only the U-5a and U-5b rates are picked up in other BLS publications. The U-5a is the overall unemployment rate that is commonly reported in the news media. The U-5b rate is the civilian unemployment rate.

The Current Employment Statistics
Program and Other BLS Surveys

The BLS's Current Employment Statistics program is a survey of 290,000 business establishments employing thirty-eight million individuals. It is conducted by the BLS in cooperation with state employment agencies. Based on payroll records, the CES provides data on the employment, hours, and earnings of employees on nonagricultural payrolls. Like the CPS, the CES is conducted monthly and covers the pay period including the twelfth day of the month. The CES counts only wage and salary workers on nonagricultural payrolls, and its concept, scope, data collection, and estimating techniques differ in several respects from those employed in the CPS. Although it is a larger sample than the CPS, in some respects the CES reflects a narrower segment of the population by excluding agricultural workers, self-employed persons, unpaid family workers, private household workers, and members of the resident armed forces. In other respects, the CES employs broader definitions than the CPS. For example, age is not a factor in the CES definition of

Table 2-1. United States Unemployment Rates

Rate	Defined as
U-1	Persons unemployed 15 weeks or longer as a percent of the civilian labor force
U-2	Job losers as a percent of the civilian labor force
U-3	Unemployed persons 25 years and older as a percent of the civilian labor force
U-4	Unemployed full-time job seekers as a percent of the full-time civilian labor force
U-5a	Total unemployed as a percent of the labor force, including the resident Armed Forces
U-5b	Total unemployed as percent of the civilian labor force
U-6	Total full-time job seekers plus 1/2 part-time job seekers plus 1/2 total part-time for economic reasons as a percent of the labor force less 1/2 part-time labor force
U-7	Total full-time job seekers plus 1/2 part-time job seekers plus 1/2 total on part-time for economic reasons plus discouraged workers as a percent of the civilian labor force plus discouraged workers less 1/2 the part-time labor force

Source: U.S. Congress, House, Committee on Government Operations, *Counting the Jobless: Problems with the Official Unemployment Rates: Hearing, March 20, 1986* (Washington, D.C.: U.S. Government Printing Office, 1986), p. 19.

"labor force." In addition, while the CPS counts an individual only once, the CES will count the same individual multiple times if that person is listed on the payrolls of more than one surveyed establishment.[5]

The BLS has several other programs that produce subnational labor force data to supplement the CPS. To the extent possible, these programs employ the concepts and definitions used in compiling national labor force data from the CPS. As previously stated, for eleven highly populated states (California, Florida, Illinois, Massachusetts, Michigan, New Jersey, New York, North Carolina, Ohio, Pennsylvania, and Texas) and the New York City and Los Angeles areas, the CPS sample size is large enough to provide reliable local area estimates. For the remaining states, the District of Columbia, and other substate areas, the labor force data are based on a combination of CPS data and a variety of other measures of the labor force, employment, and unemployment. State and local area labor force estimates generally are calculated using regression models. These models use a variety of data to represent such factors as the size of the labor force, the unemployed (both experienced and unexperienced), the employment-to-population ratio, and new entrants and reentrants to the labor force. In some cases, the modes include variables for such seasonal factors as the increase in the labor force at the end of the school year.[6]

BLS Publications

The initial announcement of the BLS's monthly labor force estimates is in "The Employment Situation," a news release typically issued the first Friday of the month following the month to which the labor estimates apply. Labor force data are officially published in *Employment and Earnings*. Each issue of *Employment and Earnings* provides both seasonally adjusted and unadjusted data. At the end of the calendar year, monthly and quarterly figures for the previous five years are revised. *Employment and Earnings* provides four categories of data. Three are relevant to the discussion here: Household Data, Establishment Data, and State and Area Labor Force Data.

The section on households is by far the largest of the four sections. It includes approximately seventy tables presenting monthly and quarterly data on employment status and on characteristics of employed and unemployed persons. All data in this section are national-level data from the household CPS. Most tables provide approximately one year of monthly data or four years of quarterly data. Selected tables provide historical trends. Data are also broken down by demographic characteristics such as age, race, sex, and so on.

The section on establishment data includes approximately eight tables. Data on the hours and earnings of employees on nonagricultural payrolls are provided. Most data are at the national level; however, one table reports data on employees on nonagricultural payrolls by state and selected area. Geographic data in this section refer to place of work. Several months of current data are generally reported, along with comparisons to the previous year and some historic data from 1933 to date. Data are calculated on the basis of the Current Employment Statistics survey of establishments. Data are provided for workers on nonagricultural payrolls by industry at the national level for approximately five hundred detailed industries (reported by Standard Industrial Classification—SIC—code). State and local area data for eight major industries are also presented in this section. Typically, monthly data for a three-month period are provided, with comparisons to data for the prior year.

The section on state and local area data consists of one lengthy table that provides data on the civilian labor force, unemployed and unemployed as a percentage of the labor force. This section provides monthly data for a three-month period. As noted above, state and local area data are compiled using several data sources, including the CPS, the LAUS, and records of state employment agencies. Places for which the CPS sample size is large enough to provide accurate data are noted. Data in this table are for place of residence, and CES place of work data are adjusted to reflect this.

Table 2-2. Labor Force Status by State and Selected Metropolitan Areas, Numbers in Thousands, September 1989

State and area	Civilian labor force	Unemployed	Percent of labor force
New York[1]	8,595.0	447.8	5.2
Albany-Schenectady-Troy	430.2	17.5	4.1
Binghamton	126.7	6.0	4.7
Buffalo	457.8	26.1	5.7
Elmira	43.6	2.2	5.1
Nassau-Suffolk	1,430.9	65.6	4.6
New York	3,927.4	227.1	5.8
New York	3,249.9	200.3	6.2
Orange County	135.4	7.3	5.4
Poughkeepsie	129.6	4.3	3.3
Rochester	506.9	20.6	4.1
Syracuse	316.4	13.7	4.3
Utica-Rome	137.7	6.5	4.7

Source: U.S. Bureau of Labor Statistics, *Employment and Earnings* (December 1989), p. 114.

Note: Data refer to place of residence.

[1] Data are obtained directly from the Current Population Survey.

Sample data from the state and local area data table for New York are given in Table 2-2. State-level data are based on the CPS. Local area data are derived from the CES. The total for the select subareas (based on the CES) provided in the table is 10,892,500. This figure exceeds the total given for all of New York State—8,595,000—which is based on the CPS. The difference is explained by the fact that the state data and the local area data are derived from different surveys.

In addition to regularly reporting these tables, *Employment and Earnings* provides quarterly averages for household or CPS survey data in its January, April, July, and October issues, and annual averages in January. For the establishment survey data, national annual averages by industry data appear in the March issue; state and area annual averages appear in the May issue.

The BLS's analyses of labor force data, along with summary data and methodological notes, often appear in *Monthly Labor Review*. Annual averages for state and local areas also are published in the BLS Bulletin series as *Geographic Profile of Employment and Unemployment*. Historical national-level data are published on a recurring basis in *Labor Force Statistics Derived from the Current Population Survey: A Databook* and in the *Handbook of Labor Statistics*. The *Handbook* includes some data by state. BLS also issues an irregular *BLS Handbook of Methods*, which provides background on the methodologies and definitions employed in the BLS's data series, including its labor force data.

Census Bureau Data

The Bureau of the Census collects a variety of information on the economic status of the population as part of both its sample surveys and its enumerative operations. The *Current Population Reports* series outlined in chapter 1 provide important intercensal information on the economic status of the population. In addition, the decennial census of population collects information on the economic status of U.S. households and individuals. The quinquennial economic censuses also canvass a variety of establishments.

The Census Bureau's intercensal data on the labor force are based on CPS data. In addition to the CPS data reported in *Employment and Earnings* and discussed earlier in this chapter, data also are reported in the *Current Population Reports* series. Labor force data appear in several of these series. For example, *Series P-20: Population Characteristics* includes reports on the farm population providing information on the employment status of the rural and farm population; occasional reports in *Series P-23: Special Studies* touch on employment topics (e.g., *Labor Force Status and Other Characteristics of Persons with a Work Disability: 1981-1988); Series P-60: Consumer Income* provides recurring coverage of the work experience of the population below the poverty level.

The Census of Population provides labor force data that are not fully compatible with the data from the CPS survey. The census typically collects data on the labor force status of the population age fifteen and older according to the following basic categories: employed (self-employed, unpaid family workers, wage and salary workers), unemployed, and not in the labor force. Respondents also report their occupation and industry of employment. Occupation is reported according to 503 categories. Industry of employment is reported according to 231 industry categories. In the 1980 census, labor force data are presented in four report series and one subject report: *Series PHC80-S2: Advanced Estimates of Social, Economic, and Housing Characteristics; Series PHC 80-4: Congressional Districts of the 98th Congress; Series PC80-1-C: General Social and Economic Characteristics; Series HC80-1-B: Detailed Housing Characteristics*; and *PC 80-2-9C: Characteristics of the Rural and Farm Related Population*. These reports provide a variety of data, including labor force status reported at varying levels of geography. (The Census of Population and Housing and other population statistics are discussed in detail in chapter 1.)

The Bureau of the Census also conducts the economic censuses. There are currently six economic censuses that are conducted quinquennially in years ending in -2 and -7. They cover agriculture, construction industries, manufactures, mining, retail trade, service industries, transportation, and wholesale trade. Unlike the Census of Population, which provides information on the labor force status and characteristics of individuals, the economic censuses provide information on employment and payrolls of business establishments in the eight broad industrial categories enumerated above.

The eight economic industrial censuses are independent programs; therefore, the exact data items available for employment and payrolls vary from series to series among the economic censuses. The range of employment data includes number of employees, production/construction workers and hours, employment by size of establishment, and employment by principal business activity. For payrolls, items available can include payroll for all employees for the entire year and first quarter, payroll for production/construction workers, and supplemental labor costs. Table 2-3 provides a breakdown of labor force data in each of the economic censuses, indicating the geographic level of coverage available.

U.S. Department of Agriculture

Supplementing the employment data of the BLS and the Census Bureau, the U.S. Department of Agriculture's National Agricultural Statistics Service (NASS) collects and disseminates information on farm employment. The NASS is one of two major statistical programs of the USDA (the other being the Economic Research Service). The NASS is charged with the preparation of estimates on production, supply, price, and other items necessary to the orderly operation of the U.S. agricultural economy. In order to prepare the estimate of farm employment, the NASS conducts the *Farm Labor* survey.

There are basic definitional and methodological differences between BLS survey operations and those employed at the NASS. This means that data from multiple sources for the U.S. agricultural work force cannot be directly compared, nor can data be aggregated for agricultural and nonagricultural employment to provide information on the total work force.

Farm Labor

The *Farm Labor* survey is a quarterly survey intended to establish estimates of agricultural employment and wage rates. The survey is based on a multiple-frame probability survey using two sampling frames. One is a list frame, which is a stratified random sample of agricultural producers likely to have hired farm workers. The second is a probability frame used to estimate employment for employers not on the list. Taken together, data from the two sampling frames are used to estimate agricultural employment and wage rates for the United States, its regions, and select states.[7]

Table 2-3. Major Data Items Relating to Employment and Payroll in Economic Censuses, by Geographic Level

Item	Retail trade	Wholesale trade	Service industries	Transportation	Manufactures	Mineral industries	Construction industries	Agriculture
Employment								
All employees	All, Z	All	All, Z	M	All	All	M	S*
Production (construction) workers/hrs.					All	All	S	
Employment size of establishment	N, Z	N	N, Z	N	All¹, Z	All	S	
Employment related to exports					S			
Employment by principal activity		N						
Payroll								
All employees, entire year	All, Z	All	All, Z	M	All	All	M	S*
All employees, first quarter	All	S	All	M		All	S	
Production (construction) workers					All		S	
Supplemental labor costs, legally required and voluntary	N	N	N		S	S		

Source: U.S. Bureau of the Census, *Guide to the 1987 Economic Censuses and Related Statistics* (Washington, D.C.: U.S. Government Printing Office, 1990), p. 3.

All = All levels (U.S., States, Sub-state, except zip codes)   M = MSAs, States, National   N = National only   S = States, National   Z = Zip codes, States   S* = States, Coverage varies
¹ No MSA summaries

For the purposes of the survey, agricultural work is defined as "work done on a farm or ranch in connection with the production of agricultural products." Employment in agricultural work is measured for self-employed, unpaid, and hired workers, as well as for employment in agricultural services. Agricultural services are defined as "agricultural work done on a farm or ranch if the provider of service is paid on a contract basis for materials, equipment, or labor."[8]

Each quarterly issue of *Farm Labor* presents data on employment, hours, and wage rates on farms in the United States. A brief analysis of the data generally precedes approximately sixteen tables. Data for the reference period, prior quarter, and same quarter of the previous year are usually provided. Select indexes, with a base of 1910-14 equals one hundred or 1977 equals one hundred, are calculated for national employment and wage rates. Some data are broken down by agricultural sector.

Wage Data

Closely allied to the labor force statistics described above is information on wages or other compensation. The various surveys outlined above collect such data along with their labor force estimates. However, a wide range of operating definitions are employed in these measures.

In *Employment and Earnings* the BLS reports hours and earnings from both the CPS household survey and the CES establishment survey. The household survey reports hours worked and median earnings aggregated for all wage and salary workers in all industries for their sole (or primary) job. Median weekly earnings of full-time wage and salary workers are also provided for fifteen occupations in six broad categories. In contrast, the establishment survey measures hours paid for by employers and average earnings of production and related workers in mining, manufacturing, and construction, and nonsupervisory employees in service industries. Earnings data from the establishment survey are also reported by some eight hundred SIC code industries. For example, the CPS household survey provides median weekly earnings of full-time wage earners and salary workers in construction trades; while the CES reports earnings data in construction by three broad subcategories (general building contractors, heavy construction—except building—and special trade contractors) and eleven detailed categories, such as electrical work and highway and street construction.

As stated above, the Census Bureau reports select data on earnings as part of its enumerations. The Census of Population and Housing collects economic data for the population age fifteen and older. The economic censuses provide a range of earnings and payroll information for the establishments in agriculture, construction industries, manufactures, mining, retail trade, service industries, transportation, and wholesale trade. Data availability is noted in Table 2-3.

Finally, the *Farm Labor* survey conducted by the NASS includes wage rates and methods of payment for hired workers. Wage rates are provided for all hired workers, as well as by method of payment (hourly, piece rate, other) and type of worker (field, livestock, supervisory, other). Wage rates are given by region and for the U.S. average.

Limitations of Labor Force Measures

As with all sample survey data, the labor force statistics described here are subject to both nonsampling and sampling errors. (These concepts are defined in chapter 1.) Given the relatively high quality of federal survey operations, the effect of nonsampling errors in technical procedures such as coding or processing are generally accepted to be negligible.[9] However, other types of nonsampling errors may play a role in the accuracy of surveys like the CPS and the *Farm Labor* survey. These include nonresponse, differences in interviewer handling of questions, and incorrect responses. Sampling errors also have a significant impact on the reliability of labor force statistics obtained from sample surveys. Sampling variances for all the labor force surveys described above generally are given in the supporting documentation or background notes to survey results, and these variances should be consulted. Specific examples of these calculations are given in chapter 8.

The definitions employed in various labor force measures are subject to a variety of criticism. This is particularly true of the concept of unemployment. The official unemployment rates (U-5a and U-5b from Table 2-1) are calculated on the basis of total unemployment (as measured by the CPS) as a percentage of either the civilian labor force or the total labor force, including resident armed forces. One school of thought argues that this definition overstates unemployment by including some persons who do not need jobs, such as students or housewives seeking part-time employment. Those who feel the present measure overstates unemployment generally argue that only breadwinners who have lost their jobs should be included in the unemployment rate.[10] The opposing viewpoint argues that the official unemployment rate understates both the problem of unemployment and the available work force. The U-7 unemployment rate, which includes both persons who work part-time for economic reasons (lack of available full-time employment) and discouraged workers, has been suggested by some members of Congress as a potentially more useful measure of stress in both the labor force and the available labor pool. A report issued by the House Committee on

Table 2-4. Range of Unemployment Rates Based on Varying Definitions of Unemployment and the Labor Force, 1970–1985

Year	U-1	U-2	U-3	U-4	U-5a	U-5b	U-6	U-7
1970	0.8	2.2	3.3	4.5	4.8	4.9	6.3	7.1
1971	1.4	2.8	4.0	5.5	5.8	5.9	7.4	8.4
1972	1.3	2.4	3.6	5.1	5.5	5.6	7.0	7.9
1973	0.9	1.9	3.1	4.4	4.8	4.9	6.2	7.0
1974	1.0	2.4	3.6	5.1	5.5	5.6	7.1	7.9
1975	2.7	4.7	6.0	8.1	8.3	8.5	10.5	11.6
1976	2.5	3.8	5.5	7.3	7.6	7.7	9.5	10.5
1977	2.0	3.2	4.9	6.6	6.9	7.1	8.8	9.8
1978	1.4	2.5	4.1	5.6	6.0	6.1	7.7	8.5
1979	1.2	2.5	3.9	5.3	5.8	5.8	7.5	8.2
1980	1.7	3.7	5.1	6.9	7.0	7.1	9.2	10.1
1981	2.1	3.9	5.4	7.3	7.5	7.6	9.8	10.8
1982	3.2	5.7	7.4	9.6	9.5	9.7	12.6	14.0
1983	3.8	5.6	7.5	9.5	9.5	9.6	12.6	13.9
1984	2.4	3.9	5.8	7.2	7.4	7.5	10.1	11.2
1985	2.0	3.6	5.6	6.8	7.1	7.2	9.6	10.6

Source: U.S. Congress, House, Committee on Government Operations, *Counting the Jobless: Problems with the Official Unemployment Rates: Hearing, March 20, 1986* (Washington, D.C.: U.S. Government Printing Office, 1986), p. 19.

Government Operations goes so far as to argue that "the U-7 unemployment rate certainly more accurately represents the hardship which is felt as a result of economic and labor market fluctuation." The report calls for greater attention to the U-7 unemployment rate.[11]

The Range of Unemployment

The various employment rates calculated by the BLS provide very different pictures of unemployment. Table 2-4 demonstrates the range of unemployment based on varying definitions of the labor force and unemployment. For the period 1970 to 1985, the U-1 rate provides the lowest unemployment rate (0.8 to 3.8 percent). This rate includes only those persons unemployed fifteen weeks or longer as a percentage of the civilian labor force. The U-7 rate provides the highest percentage (7.0 to 14.0 percent). This rate includes total full-time jobseekers as a percentage of the civilian labor force, but also makes allowances for part-time jobseekers as well as persons who work part-time for economic reasons and discouraged workers.

Undercount of certain segments of the population is a serious problem with unemployment statistics. While aggregate national-level estimates of unemployment are considered to be reliable, there are concerns over the quality of local area estimates of unemployment. Both urban and rural area estimates are influenced by undercount. Because the weighting of the CPS sample is based on the decennial census, and the census is known to undercount several groups subject to high unemployment, such as racial and ethnic minorities, the homeless, the transient, and high school dropouts, it is questionable whether the CPS can accurately reflect unemployment in these groups.[12] Methods of determining labor force participation and unemployment in rural areas also contribute to an undercount of rural unemployment. BLS definitions do not take into account characteristics of the rural labor force, including the high incidence of self-employed workers who are ineligible for unemployment insurance and whose unemployment, therefore, will go unreflected in new claims for unemployment insurance benefits. In addition, there are high percentages of discouraged workers, part-time workers for economic reasons, and unpaid family workers in rural areas. These types of stress in the rural labor force go unreflected in the current official measures of unemployment.[13]

The seasonal nature of employment also makes it difficult to compile accurate employment data. Surveys provide a snapshot of employment at a particular point in time, and that snapshot will look very different at different times in the year. Seasonal influences, such as Christmas or summer hiring, and the influx of new entrants to the job market in June of each year will look very different than the labor force data for other, perhaps slower, times of the year. In turn, these monthly or quarterly data will also look very different than annual averages that smooth out the seasonal influences. These same seasonal influences are at play in farm employment data. For example, the July survey of farm labor may yield one hundred workers, while the average for twelve monthly surveys may be forty workers. However, a total of two hundred individual workers may have been hired to generate those figures.[14] (Seasonality and seasonal adjustment are discussed in greater detail in chapter 8.)

Various definitions employed in measures of the farm labor force create ambiguities similar to those for measures of the general labor force. One farm labor expert has stated that "one truism about farm labor data is that no two sources agree on the number, distribution, or characteristics of farmworkers."[15] This is certainly due in part to the number of subtle differences in defining such key terms as *farm*, *farmworkers*, and *farm employment*. For example, some sources include employment in agricultural services as farm employment; others exclude it. Some include unpaid workers; others exclude them. Farm employment can be defined by the nature of the work or where it takes place. For example, the *Farm Labor* survey defines agricultural work as "work done on a farm." This means that work done on a farm is included in the survey; however, the same activity, if done at another location, is excluded. Conversely, other surveys, such as the CPS and CES, may define agricultural employment by the nature of the activity. The various surveys described differ not only in methodology, but in the segment of the farm labor force that they attempt to measure. It is important to remember these limitations in scope when consulting agricultural labor force statistics.

In the area of wage data, the range of available data is a cause for concern. There is a heavy emphasis on data for basic manufacturing industries. Statistical data-gathering methods have not yet caught up with the shift to a service economy. Therefore, for example, *Employment and Earnings* reports earnings for production and nonsupervisory workers in textile mills by nearly twenty subcategories; yet data for the business services industry is broken out only for advertising, services to buildings, and computer and data processing services.

Notes

1. U.S. Bureau of Labor Statistics, *BLS Handbook of Methods: Bulletin 2285* (Washington, D.C.: U.S. Government Printing Office, April 1988), p.4–5.
2. Ibid., p.5.
3. Ibid., p.6.
4. Ibid., p.3–4.
5. U.S. Bureau of Labor Statistics, "Explanatory Notes," *Employment and Earnings* (Washington, D.C.: U.S. Government Printing Office, December 1989), p.142.
6. Ibid.
7. "Sources and Reliability of Estimates," *Farm Labor*, May 1989, p.2.
8. Ibid., p.14.
9. U.S. Bureau of Labor Statistics, *Handbook of Methods*, p.10.
10. Janet Norwood, "Unemployment and Associated Measures," in *The Handbook of Economic and Financial Measures*, ed. Frank J. Fabozzi and Harry I. Greenfield (Homewood, Ill.: Dow Jones-Irwin, 1984), p.162–64.
11. U.S. Congress, House, Committee on Governmental Operations, *Counting All the Jobless: Problems with the Official Unemployment Rate* (99th Congress, 2d Session, House Report) (Washington, D.C.: U.S. Government Printing Office, 1986), p.3–4, 7.
12. Ibid., p.8.
13. Ibid.
14. Martin, *Harvest of Confusion*, p.20–21.
15. Ibid.

Bibliography

Avery, David. "Two Measures of Employment: What Can They Tell Us?" *Federal Reserve Bank of Atlanta Economic Review* (August/September 1986), p.32–39.
Daberkow, Stan, and Leslie Whitener. *Agricultural Labor Data Sources: An Update*. Economic Research Handbook Agricultural Handbook 658. Washington, D.C.: U.S. Government Printing Office, 1986.
Martin, Philip L. *Harvest of Confusion: Migrant Workers in U.S. Agriculture*. Boulder, Colo.: Westview Press, 1988.

National Commission on Employment and Unemployment Statistics. *Counting the Labor Force*. Washington, D.C.: U.S. Government Printing Office, 1979.

Norwood, Janet. "Unemployment and Associated Measures." In *The Handbook of Economic and Financial Measures*, p.143–64. Ed. Frank J. Fabozzi and Harry I. Greenfield. Homewood, Ill.: Dow Jones-Irwin, 1984.

O'Hare, William. "How to Use Income Statistics." *American Demographics* (April 1989), p.50–51.

Roth, Dennis. *Counting Migrant and Seasonal Farmworkers: A Persistent Data Void*. Congressional Research Service 85-797E. Washington, D.C.: U.S. Government Printing Office, 1985.

U.S. Bureau of Labor Statistics. *BLS Handbook of Methods: Bulletin 2285*. Washington, D.C.: U.S. Government Printing Office, April 1988.

_____ . *Employment and Earnings*. Washington, D.C.: U.S. Government Printing Office, monthly.

_____ . *Geographic Profile of Employment and Unemployment*. Washington, D.C.: U.S. Government Printing Office, annual.

_____ . *How the Government Measures Unemployment: Report 742*. Washington, D.C.: U.S. Government Printing Office, 1987.

_____ . *Labor Force Statistics Derived from the Current Population Survey: Bulletin 2096*. Washington, D.C.: U.S. Government Printing Office, irregular.

_____ . *Monthly Labor Review*. Washington, D.C.: U.S. Government Printing Office, monthly.

_____ . "State and Metropolitan Area Employment and Unemployment: Technical Note," *News* (August 18, 1987).

_____ . *Workers, Jobs, and Statistics: Questions and Answers on Labor Force Statistics: Report 698*. Washington, D.C.: U.S. Government Printing Office, 1983.

U.S. Congress. House. Committee on Governmental Operations. *Counting All the Jobless: Problems with the Official Unemployment Rate*. 99th Congress, 2d Session, House Report. Washington, D.C.: U.S. Government Printing Office, 1986.

U.S. Office of Management and Budget. *A Review of Agricultural Statistics Programs of the Bureau of the Census and U. S. Department of Agriculture*. Washington, D.C.: U.S. Government Printing Office, 1983.

Webb, John N. "Concepts Used in Unemployment Surveys," *Journal of the American Statistical Association* (March 1939), p.49–61.

What's Happening to American Labor Force and Productivity Measurements? Proceedings of a June 17, 1982 Conference. Kalamazoo, Mich.: W. E. Upjohn Institute for Employment Research, 1982.

Whitener, Leslie A. *Counting Hired Farmworkers: Some Points to Consider*. ERS-AER 524. Washington, D.C.: U. S. Government Printing Office, 1984.

United States Economic Indicators

The term "economic indicator" is often used to categorize important economic statistical series. For example, the Council of Economic Advisors uses the title *Economic Indicators* for its statistical monthly that reports data for a variety of economic data series. However, there is also a more formal and restrictive definition for the term "economic indicator." The *Dictionary of Business and Economics* defines the term as follows:

> A set of data that serves as a tool for analyzing current economic conditions and future prospects. . . . The 150 indicators currently recognized by the U.S. Bureau of Economic Analysis [BEA] are classified according to their timing in relation to the ups and downs of the business cycle, that is, whether they anticipate (lead), coincide with or lag behind general business conditions. [1]

In fact, according to the classification scheme established by the BEA, many of the statistical series reported in the Council of Economic Advisors' *Economic Indicators* are not classified as economic indicators, but are considered "Other Important Economic Measures," among them Gross National Product in current dollars and the Consumer Price Index for all urban consumers.

The Indicator System and Concept

The BEA, like the Census Bureau, is part of the Department of Commerce. It is one of the lead federal statistical agencies. The BEA is charged with the preparation, development, and interpretation of the national economic accounts. These accounts include the national income and product accounts, the national wealth accounts, the input-output accounts, personal income and related economic data, the balance of payments accounts, and the national economic accounts related to protection of the environment. This major charge is supplemented by responsibility for the preparation and analysis of measures of business activity, such as the economic indicators.

The indicators, while monitored by the BEA, are frequently not compiled by the agency. They are gathered from a number of sources, including state governments; private firms such as Standard & Poor's, and Dun and Bradstreet; associations including the Purchasing Management Association of Chicago and the American Council of Life Insurance; academic institutions such as the University of Michigan's Survey Research Center; independent research organizations such as the Conference Board and the National Bureau of Economic Research; and various federal agencies including the Bureau of the Census, the BLS, and the Board of Governors of the Federal Reserve System.

The indicator system is based on the assumption that the economy expands and contracts in a cyclical fashion. This movement is termed the *business cycle*. The indicator system attempts to gauge movements in this business cycle by tracking specific data series whose movements are expected to bear a predetermined relationship to movements in the overall economy. The relationship between a given data series and the business cycle is determined largely by comparison of the long-term past performance of the data series to that of the economy as a whole. For example, the average weekly hours of production or nonsupervisory workers in manufacturing is classified as a leading indicator at peaks, troughs, and turns in the business cycle. That is, the hours of production and nonsupervisory workers rise prior to the bottoming out of a trough in the business cycle and prior to minor upward turns in the economy. Conversely, the hours of the same workers fall prior to peaks in the economy and prior to downward turns of the business cycle. In a similar vein, the unemployment rate for persons unemployed 15 weeks or longer lags behind the business cycle. That is, this rate will continue to rise after the economy has begun a downswing, and will continue to fall once the economy has bottomed out. The Index of Industrial Production is a coincident indicator at all phases of the business cycle. Therefore, on the basis of past performance, its movements can be expected to coincide with the peaks, troughs, and turns of the economy as a whole.

Classification of Economic Indicators

In order to be classified as an economic indicator, a given economic statistic is evaluated by the BEA according to a formal weighting scheme for the six major characteristics that are outlined below (in order, from least to most heavily weighted).

Currency

Currency, or timeliness, of data refers to how promptly available and frequently reported the data are. The two criteria evaluated are periodicity and lag of release. They are the least important of all the criteria. The availability of current frequently reported data does not gauge the correlation between movements in the data and movements in the overall business cycle.

Economic Significance

Economic significance is the measure of how well understood and how important the role of the variable or process represented by a given statistic is in the overall business cycle. The evaluation of economic significance, even in a formal scheme, is ultimately a subjective judgment. It involves assessment of the importance of the variable or process in the business cycle and the breadth of coverage of the measure in terms of representing that process or variable.

Statistical Adequacy

Statistical adequacy refers to how well a given statistical series measures the variable or process in question. Seven areas are evaluated in order to evaluate the quality of the statistical methods employed in the compilation of a given measure. They are:

1. quality of the reporting system,
2. coverage (e.g., full enumeration or sample),
3. coverage of time unit (e.g., data are reported daily, monthly, quarterly, etc.),
4. measure of error,
5. frequency of revision,
6. length of series (availability of historic data to 1948 or earlier is preferable), and
7. comparability over time (e.g., the number or extent of changes in underlying definitions).

Conformity

Assessment of a measure's conformity involves the analysis of its adherence to historical business cycles: how regularly have movements of the specific measure reflected the movements of the economy at large? That is, how closely do the movements of the specific data series correlate to the peaks, troughs, and turns of the business cycle?

Smoothness

Smoothness is the measure of how promptly a cyclical turn (the peak or trough of an economic cycle) can be distinguished from the shorter, largely irregular movements in the economy that take place throughout the business cycle.

Timing

The most highly weighted characteristic is timing at revivals and recessions. That is, how consistently has the series performed at the business cycle peaks and troughs?[2]

Once a measure is given indicator status, it is evaluated for its timing at peaks, at troughs, and at all turns. In other words, although many indicators are leading, lagging, or coincident through all phases of the business cycle, some measures are classified differently at various phases in the cycle. For example, the change in the interest rate on federal funds is a leading indicator at peaks, but a lagging indicator at troughs and turns. In addition, some economic series are classified as indicators for some phases of the business cycle and unclassified for other phases. The index of spot market prices for raw industrial materials is unclassified at peaks in the cycle, but is classified as "leading" at troughs and turns. A list of the data series recognized by the BEA as economic indicators (along with their timing at peaks, troughs, and turns) is given as Table 3-1.

The Composite Indexes

In addition to classifying the individual indicators, the BEA calculates composite indexes based on the performance of select indicators. These composite indexes are constructed to maintain their timing throughout the business cycle. The composite indexes are expressed as measures of change over time, where 1982 = 100.

The leading indicators are those that anticipate movements in the economy. They are generally accepted to precede economic conditions by six to nine months. The composite index of leading indicators is composed of eleven indicators. At one time BEA also calculated indexes for four leading indicator subgroups. They were capital investment commitments (discontinued as of March 1987) inventory investment and purchasing (discontinued as of December 1988), profitability (discontinued as of November 1988), and money and financial flows (discontinued as of August 1988). The coincident indicators are those whose movements roughly coincide with the business cycle. The composite index of roughly coincident indicators is made up of four indicators.

Table 3-1. Economic Indicators as of February 1989

Series no.	Economic indicator [timing at peaks, troughs, turns]
1	Average weekly hours of production or nonsupervisory workers, manufacturing. [L,L,L]
5	Average weekly initial claims for unemployment insurance, state programs. [L,C,L]
6	Manufacturers' new orders in current dollars, durable goods industries. [L,L,L]
7	Manufacturers' new orders in 1982 dollars, durable goods industries. [L,L,L]
8	Manufacturers' new orders in 1982 dollars, consumer goods and material industries. [L,L,L]
9	Construction contracts awarded for commercial and industrial buildings, floor space. [L,C,U]
10	Contracts and orders for plant and equipment in current dollars. [L,L,L]
11	Newly approved capital appropriations, 1,000 manufacturing corporations. [U,LG,U]
12	Index of net new business formation. [L,L,L]
13	Number of new business incorporations. [L,L,L]
14	Current liabilities of business failure. [L,L,L]
15	Profits after taxes per dollar of sales, manufacturing corporations. [L,L,L]
16	Corporate profits after tax in current dollars. [L,L,L]
18	Corporate profits after tax in 1982 dollars. [L,L,L]
19	Index of stock prices, 500 common stocks. [L,L,L]
20	Contracts and orders for plant and equipment in 1982 dollars. [L,L,L]
21	Average weekly overtime hours of production or nonsupervisory workers, manufacturing. [L,C,L]
22	Ratio, corporate domestic profits after tax to total corporate domestic income. [L,L,L]
23	Index of spot market prices, raw industrial materials. [U,L,L]
24	Manufacturers' new orders in current dollars, nondefense capital goods industries. [L,L,L]
25	Change in manufacturers' unfilled orders, durable goods industries. [L,L,L]
26	Ratio, implicit price deflator to unit labor cost, nonfarm business sector. [L,L,L]
27	Manufacturers' new orders in 1982 dollars, nondefense capital goods industries. [L,L,L]
28	New private housing units started. [L,L,L]
29	New private housing units authorized by local building permits, index 1967 = 100. [L,L,L]
30	Change in business inventories in 1982 dollars. [L,L,L]
31	Change in manufacturing and trade inventories. [L,L,L]
32	Vendor performance—slower deliveries, diffusion index (percent). [L,L,L]
35	Corporate net cash flow in 1982 dollars. [L,L,L]
36	Change in manufacturing and trade inventories on hand and on order in 1982 dollars. [L,L,L]
37	Number of persons unemployed. [L,LG,U]
38	Change in manufacturers' inventories, materials and supplies on hand and on order. [L,L,L]
39	Percent of consumer installment loans delinquent 30 days or over. [L,L,L]
40	Employees on nonagricultural payrolls, goods-producing industries. [L,C,U]
41	Employees on nonagricultural payrolls. [C,C,C]
42	Number of persons engaged in nonagricultural activities. [U,C,C]
43	Unemployment rate. [L,LG,U]
44	Unemployment rate, persons employed 15 weeks and over. [LG,LG,LG]
45	Average weekly insured unemployment rate, State programs. [L,LG,U]
46	Index help-wanted advertising in newspapers. [L,LG,U]
47	Index of industrial production. [C,C,C]
48	Employee hours in nonagricultural establishments. [U,C,C]
49	Value of goods output in 1982 dollars. [C,C,C]
50	Gross national product in 1982 dollars. [C,C,C]
51	Personal income less transfer payments in 1982 dollars. [C,C,C]
52	Personal income in 1982 dollars. [C,C,C]
53	Wages and salaries in 1982 dollars, mining, manufacturing, and construction. [C,C,C]
54	Sales of retail stores in current dollars. [C,L,U]

Series no.	Economic indicator [timing at peaks, troughs, turns]
55	Personal consumption expenditures, automobiles. [L,C,C]
56	Manufacturing and trade sales in current dollars. [C,C,C]
57	Manufacturing and trade sales in 1982 dollars. [C,C,C]
58	Index of consumer sentiment. [L,L,L]
59	Sales of retail stores in 1982 dollars. [U,L,U]
60	Ratio, help-wanted advertising in newspapers to number of persons unemployed. [L,LG,U]
61	New plant and equipment expenditures by business in current dollars. [C,LG,LG]
62	Index of labor cost per unit of output, manufacturing. [LG,LG,LG]
63	Index of unit labor cost, business sector. [LG,LG,LG]
64	Compensation of employees as a percent of national income. [LG,LG,LG]
71	Manufacturing and trade inventories in current dollars. [LG,LG,LG]
72	Commercial and industrial loans outstanding in current dollars. [LG,LG,LG]
73	Index of industrial production, durable manufactures. [C,C,C]
74	Index of industrial production, nondurable manufactures. [C,L,L]
75	Index of industrial production, consumer goods. [C,C,C]
76	Index of industrial production, business equipment. [C,LG,U]
77	Ratio, manufacturing and trade inventories to sales in 1982 dollars. [LG,LG,LG]
78	Manufacturers' inventories, materials and supplies on hand and on order. [L,LG,LG]
79	Corporate profits after tax with inventory valuation and capital consumption adjustments in current dollars. [L,C,L]
80	Corporate profits after tax with inventory valuation and capital consumption adjustments in 1982 dollars. [L,C,L]
81	Ratio, corporate domestic profits after tax with inventory adjustments to total corporate domestic income. [U,L,L]
82	Capacity utilization rate, manufacturing. [L,C,U]
83	Index of consumer expectations, index 1st quarter 1966=100. [L,L,L]
84	Capacity utilization rate, materials. [L,C,U]
85	Change in money supply M1. [L,L,L]
86	Gross private nonresidential fixed investment in 1982 dollars. [C,LG,C]
87	Gross private nonresidential fixed investment in 1982 dollars, structures. [LG,LG,LG]
88	Gross private nonresidential fixed investment in 1982 dollars, producers' durable equipment. [C,LG,C]
89	Gross private residential fixed investment in 1982 dollars. [L,L,L]
90	Ratio, civilian employment to population of working age. [U,LG,U]
91	Average duration of unemployment in weeks. [LG,LG,LG]
95	Ratio, consumer installment credit outstanding to personal income. [LG,LG,LG]
96	Manufacturers' unfilled orders, durable goods industries. [L,LG,U]
97	Backlog of capital appropriations, 1000 manufacturing corporations. [C,LG,LG]
98	Percent change in producer prices for sensitive crude and intermediate materials. [L,L,L]
99	Change in sensitive material prices, smoothed. [L,L,L]
100	New plant and equipment expenditures by business in 1982 dollars. [C,LG,LG]
101	Commercial and industrial loans outstanding in 1982 dollars. [LG,LG,LG]
102	Change in money supply M2. [L,C,U]
104	Change in total liquid assets. [L,L,L]
105	Money supply M1 in 1982 dollars. [L,L,L]
106	Money supply M2 in 1982 dollars. [L,L,L]
107	Ratio, gross national product to money supply M1. [C,C,C]
108	Ratio, personal income to money supply M2. [C,LG,C]
109	Average prime rate charged by banks. [LG,LG,LG]

Table 3-1. Economic Indicators as of February 1989 (*continued*)

Series no.	Economic indicator [timing at peaks, troughs, turns]
109	Average prime rate charged by banks. [LG,LG,LG]
110	Funds raised by private nonfinancial borrowers in credit markets. [L,L,L]
111	Change in business and consumer credit outstanding. [L,L,L]
112	Net change in business loans. [L,L,L]
113	Net change in consumer installment credit. [L,L,L]
114	Discount rate on new issues of 91-day Treasury bills. [C,LG,LG]
115	Yield on long-term Treasury bills. [C,LG,LG]
116	Yield on new issues of high-grade corporate bonds. [LG,LG,LG]
117	Yield on municipal bonds, 20-bond average. [U,LG,LG]
118	Secondary market yields on FHA mortgages. [LG,LG,LG]
119	Federal funds rate. [L,LG,LG]

Source: U.S. Bureau of Economic Analysis, *Business Conditions Digest: BCD* (February 1989).

L = Leading   LG = Lagging   C = Coincident   U = Unclassified

The lagging indicators are those that reach their peaks and troughs later than the business cycle. The composite index of lagging indicators is made up of seven indicators. The components of these indexes (as of January 1992) and their sources are given in Table 3-2.

The composite indexes are calculated monthly, quarterly, and annually. The figures for a given month are released in the following month and revised in the next several months as additional data for that month become available. Thereafter, the indexes continue to be revised on a less frequent basis.

Publication

Survey of Current Business

The BEA provides preliminary access to these data in the form of a press release. The day after release, the same summary data are mailed to subscribers of the series *BEA Report: Composite Indexes of Leading, Coincident and Lagging Indicators*. Prior to April 1990, the official publication of the indicators was *Business Conditions Digest: BCD*, a monthly periodical. In *BCD*, an introductory section outlined recent changes in indicator concepts and the method of presentation. Following the introductory material was a summary table of recent data. Useful historical data covering a thirty-five-year period were also provided. *BCD* ceased publication with the March 1990 issue, and as of April 1990, the BEA incorporated scaled-down coverage of the economic indicators in *Survey of Current Business*.

Information on the economic indicators is provided in a separate section of *Survey of Current Business* titled "Business Cycle Indicators."

Table 3-2. Composite Indexes of Leading, Lagging, and Coincident Economic Indicators

Series no.	Economic indicator

Index of Leading Indicators
   1   Average weekly hours of production or nonsupervisory workers, manufacturing. (Source: U.S. Bureau of Labor Statistics [BLS])
   5   Average weekly initial claims for unemployment insurance, State programs. (Source: U.S. Department of Labor, Employment and Training Administration, seasonally adjusted by BEA)
   8   Manufacturers' new orders in 1982 dollars, consumer goods and materials industries. (Source: BEA, U.S. Bureau of the Census [Census])
  19   Index of stock prices, 500 common stocks. (Source: Standard & Poor's Corp.)
  20   Contracts and orders for plant and equipment in 1982 dollars. (Source: BEA, Census, McGraw-Hill Information Systems Co., seasonally adjusted by BEA and Census)
  29   Index of new private housing units authorized by local building permits. (Source: Census)
  32   Vendor performance, percent of companies receiving slower deliveries, diffusion index. (Source: Purchasing Management Association of Chicago)
  83   Index of consumer expectations. (Source: University of Michigan, Survey Research Center)
  92   Change in manufacturers' unfilled orders in 1982 dollars, durable goods industries, smoothed. (Source: BEA, BLS, Census)
  99   Change in sensitive materials prices. (Source: BEA, BLS, Commodity Research Bureau, Inc.)
 106   Money supply M2 in 1982 dollars. (Source: BEA, Board of Governors of the Federal Reserve System [Federal Reserve])

Index of Leading Indicators: Capital Investment Commitments Subgroup
  12   Index of Net Business formation. (Source: Dun and Bradstreet, BEA, National Bureau of Economic Research)
  20   Contracts and orders for plant and equipment in 1982 dollars. (Source: BEA, Census, McGraw-Hill Information Systems Co., seasonally adjusted by BEA and Census)
  29   Index of new private housing units authorized by local building permits. (Source: Census)

Index of Leading Indicators: Inventory Investment and Purchasing Subgroup
   8   Manufacturers' new orders in 1982 dollars, consumer goods and materials industries. (Source: BEA, Census)
  32   Vendor performance, slower deliveries diffusion index. (Source: National Association of Purchasing Management and Purchasing Management Association)
  36   Change in manufacturing and trade inventories on hand and on order in 1982 dollars. (Source: BEA, Census)
  99   Change in sensitive materials prices. (Source: BEA, BLS, Commodity Research Bureau, Inc.)

Index of Leading Indicators: Profitability Subgroup
  19   Index of stock prices, 500 common stocks. (Source: Standard & Poor's Corp.)
  26   Ratio implicit price deflator to unit labor cost, nonfarm business sector. (Source: BEA, BLS)
  80   Corporate profits after tax inventory valuation and capital consumption adjustments in 1982 dollars. (Source: BEA)

Index of Leading Economic Indicators: Money and Financial Flows Subgroup
 104   Change in total liquid assets. (Source: BEA, Federal Reserve)
 106   Money supply M2 in 1982 dollars. (Source: BEA, Federal Reserve)
 111   Change in business and consumer credit outstanding. (Source: BEA, Federal Reserve, Federal Home Loan Bank Board, Federal Reserve Bank of New York)

Table 3-2. Composite Indexes of Leading, Lagging, and Coincident Economic Indicators (*continued*)

Series No.	Economic indicator
	Index of Coincident Economic Indicators
41	Employees on nonagricultural payrolls. (Source: BLS)
47	Index of industrial production. (Source: Federal Reserve)
51	Personal income less transfer payments in 1982 dollars. (Source: BEA)
57	Manufacturing and trade sales in 1982 dollars. (Source: BEA, Census)
	Index of Lagging Economic Indicators
62	Index of labor cost per unit of output, manufacturing. (Source: BEA, Federal Reserve)
77	Ratio, manufacturing and trade inventories to sales in 1982 dollars. (Source: BEA, Census)
91	Average duration of unemployment in weeks. (Source: BLS)
95	Ratio, consumer installment credit to personal income. (Source: BEA, Federal Reserve)
101	Commercial and industrial loans outstanding in 1982 dollars. (Source: BEA, Federal Reserve, Federal Reserve Bank of New York)
109	Average prime rate charged by banks. (Source: Federal Reserve)
120	Change in Consumer Price Index for services, smoothed. (Source: BEA, BLS, Census)

Source: U.S. Bureau of Economic Analysis, *Survey of Current Business* (January 1992).

This section is divided into two parts. The first presents data for the indicators and composite indexes in tabular form. The second part provides information in chart form. Charts for the composite indexes are presented as Figures 3-1 and 3-2. The "P" and "T" at the top of the charts identify peaks and troughs in the business cycle. The solid lines plot monthly data for each of the composite indexes. The boxed arabic numerals at the right side of each chart indicate the latest month for which data are plotted. The numbers along the plotted lines indicate the length (in months) of leads (as negative numbers) or lags (as positive numbers) from turns in the business cycle. Numbers preceding each index are the reference numbers assigned to each data series. The numbers in parentheses are the reference numbers assigned to the individual indicators that are used to calculate each index.

The tables provide annual data for the previous year and monthly data for the final three months of that year and the year to date. The charts cover approximately the last twenty-five years. In each section, the composite indexes and their components are presented first, followed by the individual indicators grouped by economic process. Seven economic processes are represented in the economic indicators. "Employment and unemployment" includes measures of marginal employment adjustments, job vacancies, employment, and unemployment. "Production and income" refers to data on output and income, industrial production indexes, and capacity utilization rates. "Consumption trade, orders, and deliveries" includes orders and deliveries, and consumption and trade. "Fixed capital investment" encompasses the formation

CYCLICAL INDICATORS

Composite Indexes

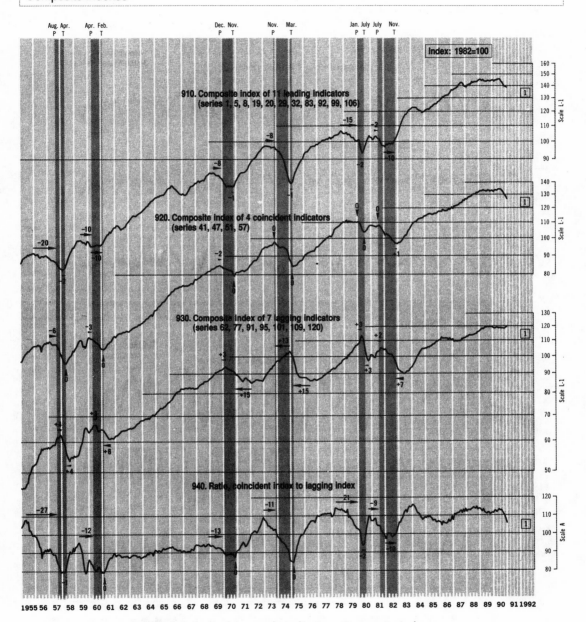

Figure 3-1. Business cycle indicators: Composite indexes
Source: U.S. Bureau of Economic Analysis, *Survey of Current Business* (February 1991).

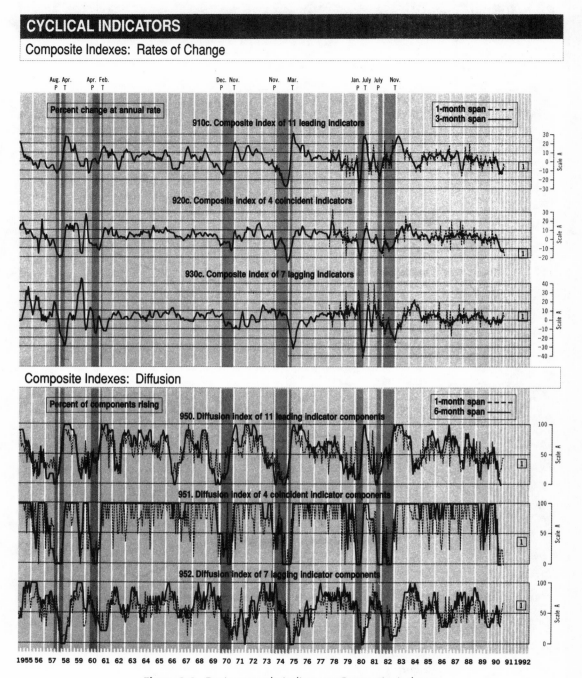

Figure 3-2. Business cycle indicators: Composite indexes—
Rates of change and diffusion
Source: U.S. Bureau of Economic Analysis, *Survey of Current Business* (February 1991).

of business enterprises, business investment commitments, business investment expenditures, and residential construction and investment. "Inventories and inventory investment" includes inventory investment and inventories on hand. "Prices, costs, and profits" includes such categories as sensitive commodity prices, Consumer Price Index for services, index of stock prices, profits and profit margins, corporate net cash flows, and unit labor costs. Lastly, "money and credit" refers to such data as money, velocity of money, credit flows, credit difficulties, bank reserves, interest rates, and outstanding debt.

Diffusion indexes and rates of change are also presented in these sections. These indexes provide information on the overall movement of the indicators by measuring the percentage of indicators that are rising. The diffusion indexes are considered to lead the overall business cycle. Rates of change for the three composite indexes are also calculated. The appendixes to *BCD* provided a variety of additional information for the indicators, including current seasonal adjustment factors for several series, experimental data and analyses including net contribution of individual components to the movement of the composite indexes, and cyclical comparisons of current and historical cycles. As of early 1992, publication plans for this information were unclear.

The BEA published an irregular supplement to *BCD*, called *Handbook of Cyclical Indicators*. The *Handbook* provided a variety of background information for the economic indicators, including definitions and methodologies for individual statistical series and an explanation of the composite indexes. The *Handbook* also offered tables covering series scores (from the weighting scheme outlined above); average time at peaks, troughs, and all turns; and measures of variability and historic data on the business cycle. However, the bulk of the *Handbook* provided historic data from 1947. Plans for updating the *Handbook* have not been announced.

Limitations

Many experts consider the utility of the economic indicators as predictive tools to be limited. There are several reasons for this. First, there is an inherent limitation in using a given data series to represent an economic process. That is, economic statistics are actually measurements of some specific phenomenon that are intended to serve as surrogates or proxies for actual forces at work in the economy. For example, one measure that might theoretically reflect changes in the level of unemployment is new claims for state unemployment insurance. The extent to which any methodology can accurately reflect the actual processes at work in the economy is limited; therefore, the ability of the economic indicator system to serve as a model for the overall business cycle is also limited. Second, despite the linkage of the historic record to indicator classification, the composite index of leading economic indicators has failed to accurately predict the actual course of the business cycle. Finally, the indicator concept is an atheoretical approach to measuring movement in the economy because the indicators are classified as such solely on the basis of the circumstantial evidence of past performance, without establishing any causal or theoretical justification for that performance. For example, the number of average weekly initial claims for unemployment insurance (state programs) is classified as leading the business cycle at peaks and turns on the basis of historical performance. However, the economic indicator system requires no causal explanation as to why a rise in unemployment should always occur prior to peaks and turns in the business cycle in order to justify that classification. Experts regard this as a serious flaw in the economic indicator concept. As early as 1947, Tjalling Koopmans characterized the concept as "measurement without theory" and criticized the "pedestrian character of the statistical devices employed." He believed that the decision not to use a theoretical approach in the analysis of business cycles "limits the value . . . of the results obtained or obtainable."[3]

More recently, Marc Levinson noted that "even believers in the Index's validity worry that its predictive value is crumbling."[4] This is due, in large part, to the shift to a service economy. Scanning the list of indicators in Table 3-1 and the list of index components in Table 3-2 reveals the weighting of the indicator system and the leading index toward manufacturing. While approximately 75 percent of jobs are now in the service sector of the economy, the only labor measure in the leading index covers production workers in manufacturing.[5] However, this problem involves more than a misplaced emphasis in the composition of the system and the indexes. Due to differences in cyclical variability, merely substituting measures for the service industries may not help. There is an additional complication in that the only detailed indicators compiled over time for service industries are those for retail trade, and—as noted above—the availability of historic data is taken into account in evaluating measures for possible inclusion in the indicators.

There are other problems with the components used in the composite index. For example, the measure of net new business formations was suspended from the indicators because "this series has deteriorated as a measure of change in the business population."[6] The series is calculated on the basis of orders for new telephone service and from Dun and Bradstreet surveys. Its suspension was due in part to the difficulty of obtaining the telephone order information following the breakup of the telephone company. In addition, the construction of this measure had been problematic because it overlooked completely the growing number of home-based businesses.

There is also criticism of the ability of the leading indicators to indicate future trends in the economy. Joseph W. Duncan, of Dun and Bradstreet, has commented in a statement to the Joint Economic Committee on the quality of the nation's economic statistics: "The leading indicators have been inconsistent, and therefore, unreliable, forecasters of economic developments."[7] There is a belief that three successive months of decline in the index are the precursor of a recession. By that token, the index predicted recessions in 1950, 1962, and 1966 that never came to pass.[8] Furthermore, while experts tend to agree that the economy entered a decline as the present decade began, the index of leading economic indicators was rising as late as June of 1990. [9]

Notes

1. Christine Ammer and Dean S. Ammer, *Dictionary of Business and Economics*, revised and expanded ed. (New York: Free Press, 1984), p.224.
2. Victor Zarnowitz and Charlotte Boschan, "Cyclical Indicators: An Evaluation and New Leading Indexes," *Business Conditions Digest: BCD*, May 1975, p.v–xix.
3. Tjalling C. Koopmans, "Measurement Without Theory," *Review of Economic Statistics*, August 1947, p.161–72.
4. Marc Levinson, "The Leading Economic Indicator Blues," *Dun's Business Month*, November 1985, p.36.
5. Alfred J. Malabre, Jr., "The Economy's Faulty Barometer," *Wall Street Journal*, December 26, 1990, p.6.
6. U.S. Bureau of Economic Analysis, *Business Conditions Digest: BCD*, December 1986, p.iii.
7. U.S. Congress, Joint Economic Committee, *The Quality of the Nation's Economic Statistics: Hearings, March 17-April 17, 1986* (Washington, D.C.: U.S. Government Printing Office, 1986), p.132.
8. Levinson, "The Leading Economic Indicator Blues," p.36.
9. Malabre, Jr., "The Economy's Faulty Barometer," p.6.

Bibliography

Ammer, Christine, and Dean S. Ammer. *Dictionary of Business and Economics*, revised and expanded ed. New York: Free Press, 1984.

Auerbach, Alan J. "The Index of Leading Indicators: 'Measurement Without Theory,' Thirty-five Years Later." *Review of Economics and Statistics* (November 1982), p.589–95.

Bingaman, Jeff. "Are Leading Indicators Misleading?" *Wall Street Journal* (June 16, 1988), p.23.

"Disagreement on Indicators." *Nation's Business* (October 1985), p.11.

"Does Anybody Really Know How the Economy Is Doing?" *Business Week* (May 6, 1985), p.128–29.

Frumkin, Norman. *Guide to Economic Indicators*. Armonk, N.Y.: M.E. Sharpe, 1990.

———. *Tracking America's Economy*. Armonk, N.Y.: M.E. Sharpe, 1987.

Hunt, Lacy. "An Antiquated, Irrelevant Index." *Wall Street Journal* (March 29, 1988).

Koopmans, Tjallings C. "Measurement Without Theory." *Review of Economic Statistics* (August 1947), p.161–72.

Levinson, Marc. "The Leading Economic Indicator Blues." *Dun's Business Month* (November 1985), p.36.

Malabre, Alfred, Jr. "The Economy's Faulty Barometer." *Wall Street Journal* (December 26, 1990), p.6.

———. "New Indicator Signals Continuing Expansion." *Wall Street Journal* (September 14, 1987), p.1.

"Not So Sad Passing of an Economic Indicator." *Business Week* (February 10, 1986), p.30.

Ortner, Robert. "Are Leading Indicators Misleading?" *Wall Street Journal* (June 16, 1988), p.23.

Parker, Robert P. "Why Economic Indicators Are Often Wrong." *Business Week* (October 17, 1983), p.168–69.

Proxmire, William. "Are Leading Indicators Misleading?" *Wall Street Journal* (June 16, 1988), p.23.

U.S. Bureau of Economic Analysis. *BEA Reports: Composite Indexes of Leading, Coincident and Lagging Indicators*. Washington, D.C.: U.S. Government Printing Office, twelve reports per year.

———. *Business Conditions Digest: BCD*. Washington, D.C.: U.S. Government Printing Office, monthly, ceased publication with March 1990.

———. *Handbook of Cyclical Indicators: A Supplement to the Business Conditions Digest*. Washington, D.C.: U.S. Government Printing Office, 1984.

———. *Survey of Current Business*. Washington, D.C.: U.S. Government Printing Office, monthly.

U.S. Congress. Joint Economic Committee. *Maintaining the Quality of Economic Data*. 99th Congress, 1st Session, Joint Committee Print. Washington, D.C.: U.S. Government Printing Office, 1981.

———. *The Quality of the Nation's Economic Statistics: Hearing, March 17-April 17, 1986*. Washington, D.C.: U.S. Government Printing Office, 1986.

Zarnowitz, Victor, and Charlotte Boschan. "Cyclical Indicators: An Evaluation and New Leading Indexes." *Business Conditions Digest: BCD* (May 1975), p.v–xix.

United States Price Indexes and Inflation Measures

Inflation measures are of interest to virtually everyone. Housewives take note of a rise in the Consumer Price Index (CPI) because it implies higher prices at the supermarket. Blue-collar workers may track the CPI because the index frequently serves as a benchmark in contract negotiations for wage increases. Likewise, retirees follow the CPI with interest because cost-of-living adjustments (COLAs) to social security benefits are pegged to this index.

While there is no single accepted definition of "inflation," it can be minimally defined as a substantial rise in the prices of a large number of goods and services or conversely, as a decline in purchasing power. To measure changes in purchasing power, the question of whose purchases to measure must be addressed.[1] There are several measures that track changes in purchasing power for various constituencies. The BLS produces both the CPI, which tracks changes in prices paid by urban consumers, and the Producer Price Index (PPI), which measures average change in selling prices received by domestic producers. The BEA calculates price deflators as part of the comprehensive system of economic accounts known as the National Income and Product Accounts (NIPAs). (The NIPAs as a whole are discussed in chapter 5.) The American Chamber of Commerce Researchers Association (ACCRA) produces a related but distinctly different measure, the Cost of Living Index. This index measures not the change in prices over time, but differences in price levels for various places at the same point in time.[2] All of these data series reveal something about purchasing power and price levels; however, in order to understand the utility of each measure, one must understand exactly what each is tracking.

Price Indexes/Price Deflators

Price indexes are typically used to measure inflation and generally measure the change in prices over a specified period of time. If, as previously noted, inflation is a substantial rise in the price levels for a large number of goods and services, to track inflation a price index must encompass the price levels for a large number of items. For example, in the case of the CPI, the price levels of some four hundred items are tracked. These items constitute the CPI market basket and are chosen to reflect the range of items in the average consumer's budget. The main components of the market basket include housing, food and beverages, transportation, clothing, and medical care.

BEA's price deflators are a by-product of the calculation of constant dollar, or inflation adjusted, estimates of production in the NIPAs. These deflators are used to provide data reflecting real growth and are expressed as the ratio of the current- to the constant-dollar estimates multiplied by 100. Sector-specific indexes from other sources are used to deflate the various sectors of production. For example, components of the CPI are used to deflate the personal consumption expenditures (PCE) component of the NIPAs.

In the fall of 1991, the BEA announced a benchmark revision of the NIPAs that changed that basic aggregate of production from Gross National Product to Gross Domestic Product. Gross National Product (GNP) is defined as the market value of goods and services produced by labor and property supplied by residents of the United States. GNP includes and excludes production activity on the basis of ownership of capital and can include production occurring outside the United States. Gross Domestic Product (GDP) defines a nation's production as domestic output and is a more internationally comparable data series. In addition, the benchmark revision changed the base year of the price deflators from 1982 to 1987. (Further explanation of this shift is provided in chapter 5.)

U.S. Bureau of Labor Statistics

As one of its major mandates, the BLS is responsible for the concept, analysis, and publication of data relating to prices and family expenditures. To fulfill that mandate, the BLS collects data on producer prices, international price indexes, consumer expenditures and income, and consumer prices. The BLS's work in the areas of consumer prices and producer prices is particularly relevant to the discussion here.

Consumer Price Index

The CPI is perhaps the most widely known measure of inflation. It was devised during World War I to help set wages in the shipbuilding industry. It has since been almost universally adopted as an escalator for automatic COLAs for union wages and social security benefits. The CPI is also used to deflate or adjust a number of other economic data series for inflation.[3]

According to the BLS, the CPI is "a measure of the average change in prices paid by urban consumers for a fixed market basket of goods and services. . . . [T]he CPI uses a fixed market basket to hold the base-period living standard constant." The CPI is calculated on the basis of prices for a sample of food, shelter and fuels, transportation, medical services, and other goods and services that urban consumers buy for day-to-day living. Price change is measured by repricing essentially the same market basket of goods and services at regular time intervals and by comparing aggregate costs with the costs of the same items in a selected base period. Currently, the base period for the CPI is 1982-84 equals 100. Price levels for other periods are expressed as a percentage of the level of the base period. For example, the CPI for 1990 is 130.7. This means that the aggregate price increase for the period from 1982-84 is 30.7 percent.[4]

Price surveys for the CPI are currently conducted in eighty-five primary sampling units (PSUs). Each PSU is made up of central cities, suburbs, and urbanized areas within two miles of a selected county or group of contiguous counties with similar demographic and economic characteristics.[5] On a monthly basis, BLS representatives collect prices in all eighty-five PSUs for items in the CPI market basket. Items that make up the CPI market basket fall into eight groups: food and beverages, fuel and utilities, household services and furnishings, apparel and upkeep, transportation, medical care, entertainment, and other commodities and services. Each of these components has a separate survey with its own sample design.[6]

The results of the BLS's price surveys are used to calculate the CPI. The CPI is actually a family of price indexes covering prices paid by urban consumers. There are two national-level (U.S. cities average) indexes that summarize price levels for all goods and services. They are the Consumer Price Index-Urban Wage Earners and Clerical Workers (CPI-W), which measures prices paid by blue-collar wage earners and clerical workers in urban areas, and the Consumer Price Index-All Urban Consumers (CPI-U), which encompasses a broader range of urban workers, including wage earners and clerical workers, along with urban salaried workers, the self-employed, the retired, and the unemployed.[7] As part of the CPI family, specialized indexes are also calculated for a wide variety of commodities and services (by region and size of city) and for twenty-nine separate local areas.[8]

The weighting pattern and composition of the CPI market basket is based on studies of consumer and family expenditures. Over the years, a number of surveys and studies have been conducted by the BLS to help refine the composition of the CPI. The ongoing Consumer Expenditure Survey and the Point-of-Purchase Survey are used to monitor and refine both the composition of the CPI and sampling procedures and outlets. The Consumer Expenditure Survey is conducted to provide timely and detailed information on the consumption patterns of different kinds of families. Data from the Consumer Expenditure Survey provide the basis for revising the weights and pricing samples for the CPI. The Point-of-Purchase Survey is conducted annually (usually in April) to determine demographic and socioeconomic characteristics, and buying patterns of urban households, as well as the outlets from which they made purchases.[9]

Producer Price Index

Just as the CPI measures changes in the prices paid by urban consumers, the PPI measures changes in the selling prices received by domestic producers for their output. Currently, the base year for the PPI is 1982 equals 100. The information used in calculating the PPI is derived from systematic sampling of producers in approximately five hundred mining and manufacturing industries. The PPI is one of the oldest economic time series compiled by the federal government. It was first published in 1902 as the Wholesale Price Index (WPI) and was originally intended to measure prices received for goods sold in the primary markets of this country. The old WPI became outmoded over time, and in 1978 the index was drastically revised and renamed the Producer Price Index. The name change was spurred by confusion over and change in the concept of "wholesale." The adoption of the term *producer prices* was intended to stress that the prices being measured are those received by producers from whomever made the first purchase of an item.[10]

As with the CPI, the PPI is not a single price index, but an entire family of indexes. The program includes price indexes for approximately eight thousand items or groups of items produced by nearly five hundred mining and manufacturing industries. It also provides price indexes by type of product and end use, and major aggregate measures of price change by stage of process. Prices are collected by field economists from establishments that have volunteered to provide data for use in compiling the PPI.[11]

BLS Publications

Two types of BLS publications are of interest to users of the CPI and PPI. One category of publications provides access to the data themselves. The other includes handbooks and guides that provide background information, such as key definitions, methodology, and data limitations.

The CPI for a given period is published first in a news release issued between the twentieth and the twenty-fifth of the following month. *CPI Mailgram* then provides selected data within twenty-four hours of release. Summary tables are published in the *Monthly Labor Review* the following month; shortly thereafter, detailed data appear in the monthly publication *CPI Detailed Report*.

The *CPI Detailed Report* provides data on the CPI for the United States. A variety of tables provide data, such as aggregate rates of change in consumer prices, and rates of change for specific expenditure categories, commodities, and cities. Most of the data are for the current reference period only; select annual figures and short-term trends are provided.

The PPI is usually issued in the middle of the month following the period of coverage. As with the CPI, the first release of the PPI is in the form of a news release with summary data. Brief tables are published in the *Monthly Labor Review*. A detailed report, *Producer Price Indexes*, is printed approximately one month after the news release.

Producer Price Indexes provides data on change in producer prices for the United States. This report provides detailed data on change in prices by commodity and commodity group, as well as by stage of processing (for finished consumer goods and capital equipment, intermediate supplies and components, and crude materials). Select annual figures and short-term trends are provided.

The BLS publishes background information that aids in the interpretation and use of its price indexes. The *Monthly Labor Review* frequently features articles on statistical methods and revision of the indexes. The *BLS Handbook of Methods* provides detailed explanations of the BLS's statistical series. The section "Prices and Living Conditions" highlights both the PPI and CPI. Topics covered include background such as definitions and history; survey description including procedures for data collection and survey methodology; estimating procedures including weights and index calculation; presentation of data including analysis, classification schemes, and uses; and limitations of data including precision of estimates and statistical limitations of the indexes.

U.S. Bureau of Economic Analysis
Price Deflators

Augmenting the price indexes of the BLS, the BEA produces price deflators that provide information on inflation and price levels. These measures are prepared as part of the BEA's charge to provide a clear picture of the U.S. economy through the preparation, development, and interpretation of the National Income and Product Accounts.

NIPA Price Deflators

The most comprehensive price indexes available are the BEA's price deflators. These indexes are widely used as generalized measures of inflation. The price deflators are a by-product of the preparation of constant dollar estimates of production in the NIPAs. They are expressed as the ratio of the current dollar estimates to the constant dollar estimates multiplied by 100. In addition to shifting the basic aggregation of production from GNP to GDP, BEA's benchmark revision will shift the base year for the deflators from 1982 to 1987.

Sector-specific indexes are used to deflate the various components of production. Components of the CPI are used to deflate the PCE component of the GNP. Similarly, components of the PPI are used to adjust gross private domestic investment (which includes such business expenditures as capital equipment and raw materials), and so on, for the other components of the NIPAs. The PCE price deflator measures the change in prices for the personal consumption portion of the NIPAs and is the closest of the BEA deflators to the CPI. However, it differs from the CPI in several ways. The PCE price deflator measures the change in prices of items actually purchased by consumers rather than using a fixed market basket like the CPI. The PCE price deflator also excludes some items that CPI includes such as anything not newly produced, like used cars.[12]

The specialized price deflators are then aggregated to produce the overall implicit price deflator. The BEA has introduced major changes to its deflators as part of the benchmark revision. The implicit price deflator will now be based on the GDP rather than the GNP. In addition, the deflators will now be called "Quantity and Price Indexes." As of January 1992, few of these indexes have appeared but once the system is in place for each component of the NIPAs (personal consumption expenditures, gross private domestic investment, export of goods and services, and so forth), the BEA will now produce four basic types of price indexes: current dollar indexes, quantity indexes, price indexes, and implicit price deflators. The current dollar indexes express unadjusted change in value since 1987. There are three separate quantity indexes and three separate price indexes. The first is produced with fixed 1987 weights. That is, the index is produced assuming constant weighting that reflects the composition of the production component in 1987. The second, chain-type annual weight index, will be weighted to reflect the composition of output (on either a quantity or value basis) for the preceding and current year. An alternate index will use benchmark year weights. Finally, the implicit price deflator will reflect production adjusted for inflation (as well as changes in composition) with a base year of 1987.

To illustrate the various measures of inflation in the NIPAs and the concept of weighting and chain-type indexes, data for the GNP implicit price deflator, its component specialized indexes, and the fixed-weight and chain price indexes are given in Table 4-1. (The old GNP system is used because sufficient new benchmark data were not yet available as this volume appeared.) The sector-specific components are personal consumption expenditures, gross private domestic investment, net exports of goods and services, and government purchases of goods and services. These specialized deflators provide differing pictures of inflation. For example, as shown in Table 4-1, the GNP implicit price deflator for the period 1982 to 1986 (which expresses the change in prices for that period, including both inflation and changes in the composition of the GNP) was 13.8 percent. For the same period, the change in the fixed-weight index for the GNP was 14.9 percent (which measures inflation using constant weights that reflect the composition of the GNP in 1982). The chain version of the fixed-weight index for 1986 was 2.5 percent (which reflects only the change in prices between 1985 and 1986, again using constant weights based on the composition of the GNP in 1985).

BEA Publications

All of the BEA's new quantity and price indexes will be published as part of the NIPAs. Some fifteen tables provide information on the various indexes. The NIPAs are published officially in *Survey of Current Business* and appear on a quarterly basis, with the most recent annual revision published every July. As with the other NIPA components, historical data and background information are provided in the biennial *Business Statistics* and in *National Income and Product Accounts: Statistical Tables*, which is published approximately every five years.

Cost of Living Index

The ACCRA publishes an index that provides an interesting contrast to the measures profiled above. The ACCRA is the professional association of city, regional, and state researchers, usually employed by chambers of commerce or economic development organizations involved in applied community research. Its purpose is to exchange information and technical ideas on industrial, economic, and technical research. The ACCRA's Cost of Living Index (formerly known as the Inter-city Cost of Living Index) is a collaborative research effort intended to provide a useful and reasonably accurate measure of intercity cost-of-living differences. The ACCRA index does not measure inflation (or price change over time); instead, each quarter the index provides a comparison of price levels in selected U.S. cities.

Table 4-1. Components of GNP Implicit Price Deflators and Fixed-Weight Price Indexes

	Implicit price deflators (1982 = 100)			Fixed weighted price indexes 1982 weights (1982 = 100)			Chain price indexes (Percent change from preceding period)		
	1986	1987	1988	1986	1987	1988	1986	1987	1988
Gross national product	113.8	117.4	121.3	114.9	118.9	123.9	2.5	3.3	3.7
Personal consumption expenditures	114.3	119.6	124.2	115.3	120.6	125.6	2.7	4.6	4.0
Durable goods	105.6	108.2	109.4	106.5	110.1	111.9	1.1	3.0	1.7
Nondurable goods	107.3	112.2	116.6	107.8	112.6	117.3	0	4.5	4.1
Services	122.4	128.7	134.5	123.1	129.2	135.2	5.0	5.1	4.6
Gross private domestic investment									
Fixed investment	102.9	103.9	105.7	105.7	107.4	111.2	2.2	2.0	2.9
Nonresidential	99.3	98.9	100.2	104.2	105.2	109.0	2.0	1.1	2.5
Structures	106.9	108.9	114.3	101.6	101.2	107.1	1.2	1.2	4.8
Producers' durable equipment	96.1	95.2	95.5	105.9	107.8	110.2	2.5	1.1	1.6
Residential	111.1	115.2	119.3	110.9	115.0	119.1	2.5	3.8	3.6
Net exports of goods and services									
Exports	99.8	99.5	103.2	103.6	105.7	111.3	−0.6	1.8	4.9
Imports	93.7	99.0	102.5	94.0	110.6	105.8	0.3	6.9	5.4
Government purchases of goods and services	114.5	118.3	123.3	115.5	119.3	124.9	2.0	2.9	3.8
Federal	109.7	112.3	115.9	110.6	112.9	117.4	0.4	1.4	2.3
National defense	110.2	111.1	114.0	111.1	113.5	117.4	0.9	1.2	2.2
Nondefense	108.1	116.3	123.2	109.4	111.6	117.6	−0.9	2.0	2.5
State and local	118.3	122.9	128.7	119.2	124.0	130.1	3.2	3.9	4.8

Source: U.S. Bureau of Economic Analysis, *Survey of Current Business* (July 1990), p. 88–97.

To compile the ACCRA index each quarter, participating chambers of commerce price a selection of items in their local areas. The items that serve as the basis for the index are chosen to reflect different categories of consumer expenditures. From these prices, an All-Items Index is constructed that reflects the relative price levels for consumer goods and services in participating cities (both aggregate and for select items) as compared with the national average of 100 for all participating cities (metropolitan and nonmetropolitan). As participation in the survey is voluntary, the number and mix of cities represented in the index may change from quarter to quarter.[13]

Table 4-2 compares CPI data for selected local areas with the Cost of Living, All-Items Index data for select participating cities. As noted above, the CPI measures the change in prices over time. Although the CPI is calculated for a limited number of metropolitan areas, these geographic indexes measure the change in prices over time for each area and cannot

Table 4-2. Consumer Price Index for All Urban Consumers, Selected Areas, and ACCRA Cost of Living Index, All-Items Index, 1989

CPI-U (1982–1984 = 100)	1986	1987	1988
Baltimore, MD MSA	122.8	127.6	133.8
Dallas–Fort Worth, TX CMSA	118.7	119.1	118.2
Los Angeles–Anaheim–Riverside, CA CMSA	125.5	133.5	140.6
San Francisco–Oakland–San Jose, CA CMSA	134.9	140.5	146.6

Cost of Living Index (US City Average = 100)	1st qtr. 1986	1st qtr. 1987	1st qtr. 1988
Baltimore, MD	105.9	105.2	104.1
Dallas, TX	113.5	106.6	105.8
Los Angeles	112.3	115.7	117.0
San Jose, CA	111.2	117.8	117.9

Sources: U.S. Bureau of the Census, *Statistical Abstract of the United States: 1990* (Washington, D.C.: U.S. Government Printing Office, 1990), p. 473. American Chamber of Commerce Researchers Association, *Inter-city Cost of Living Index*, 1st qtr. 1986, 1st qtr. 1987, 1st qtr. 1988, section 1 (Louisville, Ky.: ACCRA).

be used to measure differences in price levels for areas relative to one another.[14] Conversely, the ACCRA index takes as its base the national average of prices of selected items at a specific point in time so that costs for geographic areas can be compared to that average and to one another. However, with this type of indexing, no time series comparison is possible.

The ACCRA index has distinct limitations. It is not valid to treat percentage differences between cities as exact measures because the number of items priced is rather limited. According to ACCRA documentation, spreads of 3 percent or less in the All-Items Index may not represent statistically significant differences and may not even correctly show which city is more expensive. Differences of more than 3 percent in the All-Items Index can be considered to represent actual intercity differences in the costs of consumer goods and services, but the percentage difference in such cases should be considered a reasonable indication, rather than a precise measure, of the extent of the difference.[15]

ACCRA Publications

The Cost of Living Index is published quarterly in a publication entitled *Cost of Living Index*. In addition to the All-Items Index for participating cities for the reference period, six component indexes—grocery items, housing, utilities, transportation, health care, and miscellaneous goods and services—and the individual commodity prices that provide the basis for the index are also included.

Comparison of Measures of Inflation

Each of the four major measures of price change outlined above gives a different picture of inflation. Table 4-3 presents data for the CPI-U (U.S. cities average), the PPI (finished goods), the GNP implicit price deflator, and the PCE price deflator. From 1987 to 1988, for example, the CPI rose 4.1 percent; the PPI rose 2.5 percent; the GNP deflator rose 3.3 percent; while its derivative, the PCE deflator, rose 3.9 percent. From 1978 to 1979, the growth rates were 11.3 percent for the CPI, 11.2 percent for the PPI, 8.9 percent for the GNP deflator, and 9.2 percent for the PCE deflator. These differences illustrate the range of inflation depending on whose purchases or what prices are tracked and how. Also, these differences take on public policy implications when employed in cost-of-living adjustment of wages, pensions, or social security benefits. As Walter Heller noted

> [T]he choice of an index makes a difference in the rate of inflation itself. For example, the CPI is typically used to make cost-of-living adjustments in wages. If, as alleged, it overstates the increase in the cost of living, the phantom increase in inflation gets woven into the pattern of wages and prices and hence into the fabric of inflation itself. In a sense, the medium becomes the message, or more to the point in this case, the measure of inflation becomes the medium for escalating inflation. Statistics become substance. Without them, the correction for the inequity of inflation would be impossible. But until they are adjusted to measure inflation's burden more precisely, they may well over-correct for those burdens.[16]

Further, because investors and corporate decision makers track CPI closely and base financial decisions in some degree on its movements, CPI's broader influence on the economy is not inconsequential.

Limitations in Inflation Measures

Each of the measures of inflation discussed here is limited by the methodology and definitions by which it was compiled. Each was developed and produced by data analysts for specific purposes, and therefore some measures are appropriate for certain types of comparisons and not for others.

The CPI, for example, is widely used to measure inflation, as well as changes in the cost of living; however, the methodology employed in the compilation of the CPI places distinct limitations on its usefulness for these purposes. As noted above, the indexes for select local areas

Table 4-3. Annual Averages for CPI for All Urban Consumers, Producer Price Index (Finished Goods), GNP Implicit Price Deflator, PCE Price Deflator

	CPI-U (1982–84 = 100)	PPI (finished goods) (1982 = 100)	GNP deflator (1982 = 100)	PCE deflator (1982 = 100)
1975	53.8	58.2	59.3	59.2
1976	56.9	60.8	63.1	62.6
1977	60.6	64.7	67.3	66.7
1978	65.2	69.8	72.2	71.6
1979	72.6	77.6	78.6	78.2
1980	82.4	88.0	85.7	86.6
1981	90.9	96.1	94.0	94.6
1982	96.5	100.0	100.0	100.0
1983	99.6	101.6	103.9	104.1
1984	103.9	103.7	107.7	108.1
1985	107.6	104.7	110.9	111.6
1986	109.6	103.2	113.8	114.3
1987	113.6	105.4	117.4	119.8
1988	118.3	108.0	121.3	124.5

Sources: U.S. Bureau of Labor Statistics, *Handbook of Labor Statistics: Bulletin 2340* (Washington, D.C.: U.S. Government Printing Office, 1989), p. 475, 488. U. S. Bureau of the Census, *Statistical Abstract of the United States: 1990* (Washington, D.C.: U.S. Government Printing Office, 1990), p. 470, 476, 480–81. U.S. Bureau of Economic Analysis, *National Income and Product Accounts, 1929–1982: Statistical Tables* (Washington, D.C.: U.S. Government Printing Office, 1986), p. 328.

may not be used for geographic comparisons in cost of living, only for tracking the change in prices for those areas over time. It is also critical to remember what prices or whose purchases are being tracked. The CPI is specifically intended to measure changes in prices for all urban consumers. Therefore, the relationship between changes in the CPI and inflation for rural or nonmetropolitan areas, or for specific segments of the population, urban or rural, is unknown.[17] The construction of the CPI may or may not allow it to accurately reflect changes in prices paid by rural or nonmetropolitan workers, or by specific demographic subgroups of the population with potentially different purchasing patterns, such as the elderly.

Further, because the CPI is based on the concept of a fixed market basket of goods and services, its usefulness is limited in several significant ways. First, it cannot be considered a true cost-of-living index because it does not attempt to take into account consumer behavior or the changes in buying patterns that are likely to occur in response to changes in prices. For example, when prices rise consumers are likely to make substitutions of cheaper products (or to do without) to accommodate these higher prices.[18] In addition, the CPI does not take into account changes in quality of items in the market basket. That is, when the quality of a product changes—for better or worse—whether or not the price changes, there is a change in value for dollar that goes unreflected in the CPI. That change can take many forms. Prices may rise as quality goes up, or fall as quality goes down; however, there are also many instances where quality improves even as prices fall due to the implementation of improved production methods (changes in price and quality in the microcomputer market provide an excellent example of this phenomenon). The CPI is not weighted to account for this complex and important process and therefore, does not assess the true change in price, only the nominal change. This problem is perhaps CPI's most serious flaw.[19]

Notes

1. Joel Popkin, "Measures of Inflation," in *The Handbook of Economic and Financial Measures*, ed. Frank J. Fabozzi and Harry I. Greenfield (Homewood, Ill.: Dow Jones-Irwin, 1984), p.343.
2. The BLS has experimental interarea price indexes under development. Due to their experimental nature, these indexes have been omitted from this chapter.
3. U.S. Bureau of Labor Statistics, *BLS Handbook of Methods* (Washington, D.C.: U.S. Government Printing Office, April 1988), p.154.
4. Ibid., p.154–55.
5. U.S. Bureau of Labor Statistics, *Handbook of Labor Statistics: Bulletin 2340* (Washington, D.C.: U.S. Government Printing Office, 1989), p.470.
6. U.S. Bureau of Labor Statistics, *BLS Handbook of Methods*, p.161–62.
7. Ibid., p.162.
8. U.S. Bureau of Labor Statistics, *Handbook of Labor Statistics: Bulletin 2340*, p.470.
9. Ibid., p.156, 163–64.
10. Ibid., p.125.
11. Ibid., p.125–26.
12. Philip Cagan and Geoffrey H. Moore, *The Consumer Price Index: Issues and Alternatives* (Washington, D.C.: American Enterprise Institute, 1981), p.47–48; and Walter W. Heller, "Economic Policy for Inflation: Shadow, Substance, and Statistics" in U.S. Bureau of the Census, *Reflections of America: Commemorating the Statistical Abstract Centennial* (Washington, D.C.: U.S. Government Printing Office, December 1980), p.82.
13. American Chamber of Commerce Researchers Association, *Cost of Living Index* (Louisville, Ky.: quarterly).
14. U.S. Bureau of Labor Statistics, *Revising the Consumer Price Index: Report 734* (Washington, D.C.: U.S. Government Printing Office, November 1986), p.4.
15. American Chamber of Commerce Researchers Association, *Cost of Living Index*.
16. Heller, "Economic Policy for Inflation," p.83–84.
17. U.S. Bureau of Labor Statistics, *BLS Handbook of Methods*, p.158.
18. U.S. Bureau of Labor Statistics, *Revising the Consumer Price Index*, p.1.
19. Popkin, "Measures of Inflation," p.350.

Bibliography

American Chamber of Commerce Researchers Association. *Cost of Living Index*. Louisville, Ky.: quarterly.

Cagan, Philip and Geoffrey H. Moore. *The Consumer Price Index: Issues and Alternatives*. Washington, D.C.: American Enterprise Institute, 1981.

Gaddie, Robert, and Maureen Zoller. "New Stage of Process Price System Developed for the Producer Price Index." *Monthly Labor Review* (April 1988), p.3–16.

Greenwald, Douglas. *Encyclopedia of Economics*. New York: McGraw-Hill, 1982, p.313–21.

Heller, Walter W. "Economic Policy for Inflation: Shadow, Substance, and Statistics." In U.S. Bureau of the Census, *Reflections of America: Commemorating the Statistical Abstract Centennial*. Washington, D.C.: U.S. Government Printing Office, December 1980.

Marcoot, John L., and Richard C. Blair. "The Revised Consumer Price Index: Changes in Definitions and Availability." *Monthly Labor Review* (July 1986), p.15–23.

Mason, Charles, and Clifford Butler. "New Basket of Goods and Services Being Priced in Revised CPI." *Monthly Labor Review* (January 1987), p.3–22.

"Measuring Inflation: Is a New Index Needed?" *Congressional Quarterly Weekly Report* (August 22, 1987), p.1948–49.

O'Hara, Frederick M., Jr., and Robert Sicignano. *Handbook of Economic and Financial Measures*. Westport, Conn.: Greenwood Press, 1984.

Popkin, Joel. "Measures of Inflation." In *The Handbook of Economic and Financial Measures*, p.343–57. Ed. Frank J. Fabozzi and Harry I. Greenfield. Homewood, Ill.: Dow Jones-Irwin, 1984.

Ross, Irwin. "Misleading Government Data: Why Statistics May Mislead." *Current* (November 1986), p.19–21.

Schmidt, Mary Lynn. "Comparison of the Revised and the Old CPI." *Monthly Labor Review* (November 1987), p.3–6.

Slater, Courtney. "A New Market Basket." *American Demographics* (January 1987), p.4–6.

U.S. Bureau of Economic Analysis. *Business Statistics*. Washington, D.C.: U.S. Government Printing Office, biennially.

_____ . *National Income and Product Accounts: Statistical Tables*. Washington, D.C.: U.S. Government Printing Office, quinquennially.

_____ . *Survey of Current Business*. Washington, D.C.: U.S. Government Printing Office, monthly.

U.S. Bureau of Labor Statistics. *BLS Handbook of Methods*. Washington, D.C.: U.S. Government Printing Office, April 1988.

_____ . *The Consumer Price Index: 1987 Revision: Report 736*. Washington, D.C.: U.S. Government Printing Office, January 1987.

_____ . *CPI Detailed Report*. Washington, D.C.: U.S. Government Printing Office, monthly.

_____ . *CPI Mailgram*. Springfield, Md.: National Technical Information Service, monthly.

_____ . *Monthly Labor Review*. Washington, D.C.: U.S. Government Printing Office, monthly.

———. *Producer Price Indexes*. Washington, D.C.: U.S. Government Printing Office, monthly.

———. *Revising the Consumer Price Index: Report 734*. Washington, D.C.: U.S. Government Printing Office, November 1986.

———. *Using the Consumer Price Index for Escalation: Report 732*. Washington, D.C.: U.S. Government Printing Office, October 1986.

U.S. Congressional Budget Office. *Indexing with the Consumer Price Index: Problems and Alternatives*. Washington, D.C.: U.S. Government Printing Office, June 1981.

"Which Price Indicator Do You Believe?" *Business Week* (May 14, 1979), p.121–22.

Gross National Product and Other Measures of Production

Production or output is perhaps the primary gauge of the state of the economy. Several statistical series measure some aspect of production including the Federal Reserve's Index of Industrial Production, and input-output measures compiled by the Census Bureau and the BEA. However, the GNP is the most widely used and comprehensive measure of U.S. production. The GNP has primarily been an analytical tool for assessing present economic performance and predicting future economic activity. Although its analytical uses are its primary function, the GNP has additional secondary applications; for example, it is used to develop benchmarks in the federal budget process. Starting in January 1992, the BEA is in the process of shifting its emphasis from GNP to GDP, or Gross Domestic Product. GDP is now the basic aggregate of production.

Measurement of a nation's output requires a complex methodology. Dozens of statistical series, compiled by numerous sources—public and private—are analyzed, adjusted, and merged in order to produce estimates of production for the NIPAs. Due to the scale and complexity of this task, these data are subject to several statistical limitations.

Gross National Product

The BEA has as its major charge the production of estimates of production. Until 1992, the primary measure of production was the GNP. The *Statistical Abstract of the United States* defines GNP as "the total national output of goods and services valued at market prices."[1] More specifically, the BEA defines it as follows:

. . . the market value of goods and services produced by labor and property supplied by residents of the United States. It is the sum of purchases of goods and services by persons and government, gross private domestic investment (including change in business inventories), and net exports (exports less imports). GNP excludes business purchases of goods and services on current account.[2]

In general, the value of goods and services reflected by the GNP is that of final sale goods or services only and not the value of their components. The value of products used in further production is reflected in the value of the final sale product, or in inventory change, and therefore is not counted twice. For example, the market value of automobiles is counted, while the purchase of steel used to make automobiles is not.

Gross Domestic Product

Although the GNP has been the most widely used measure of U.S. production, BEA has shifted its emphasis from GNP to GDP or Gross Domestic Product. The GDP represents a portion of the GNP. Where the GNP aggregates national production, the GDP measures domestic output. The GDP includes the total value of U.S. production "within its physical borders." That is, the GNP is the GDP plus the value of production based on national ownership of capital, but occurring throughout the rest of the world. The determining factor for inclusion of production in the GNP is solely the ownership of underlying capital; however, the GDP further includes or excludes production based on the location of the activity.[3] This makes GNP figures inappropriate for comparison to the GDP figures frequently reported by foreign nations. There can be a significant difference between the two measures; for example, the U.S. GNP for 1986 was $3,713.3 billion, while the GDP was $3,683.5 billion.[4] The issue of international comparability is a prime motivation for BEA's changeover.

The National Income and Product Accounts

The GDP is part of a comprehensive system of macroeconomic statistics known as National Income and Product Accounts (NIPAs). The NIPAs provide a picture of the complex organization of the national economy, its income and output. More simply put:

The fundamental aim of national income accounting is to provide a coherent picture of the Nation's economy . . . [by answering two questions:] what is the output of the economy—its size, its composition, and its use? Second, what is the economic process or mechanism by which this output is produced and distributed?[5]

While the BEA is chiefly responsible for the compilation of the GDP and the NIPAs, the source data used in its calculation are collected largely by other sources for other purposes and then reported to the BEA. Among the federal agencies collecting data used in NIPA calculations are the U.S. Department of Agriculture, the Treasury department, the Office of Management and Budget, the Census Bureau, the Internal Revenue Service, the Social Security Administration, and the BLS. Private sources also provide data for the calculation of the NIPAs. These sources include trade associations, businesses, labor organizations, and welfare, educational, and religious groups. In addition, different data sources are used in the compilation of the quarterly and annual estimates of production.

This diverse body of data (compiled by a variety of statistical techniques and varying in reliability) must then be processed by the BEA. This procedure involves analyzing and adjusting the data, filling in gaps in information, and reconciling discrepancies in data. Production figures are also seasonally adjusted and are expressed in both current and constant dollars. (For further explanation of seasonal adjustment and current or constant dollar estimates, see chapter 8.)

All NIPA figures are estimates. The preliminary estimates for a given quarter are published in the month following the end of that quarter. As additional and superior data become available, figures are recalculated, and revised estimates are issued. The first two revised estimates are issued in the two months immediately following the release of the initial preliminary estimate. Figures for the most recent three years are also revised annually. A comprehensive benchmark revision is usually completed every five years, the most recent being 1992. The latest revised estimates are considered more accurate than any earlier estimates for a given period because they are based on more detailed and accurate source data.

The five main accounts in the NIPA system are the (1) National Income and Product Account, (2) Personal Income and Outlay Account, (3) Government Receipts and Expenditures Account, (4) Foreign Transactions Account, and (5) Gross Savings and Investment Account. The NIPAs employ a double-entry bookkeeping system. Each economic transaction recorded in the NIPAs represents the exchange of one good, service, or financial asset for another. Therefore, each transaction is theoretically recorded twice in the accounts in order to represent each side of the exchange. The two sides of the transactions (and the accounts) are commonly referred to as the product side, or right-hand side, and the income side, or left-hand side. These two sides can be considered as two different methodologies for calculating the same economic variable. Ideally, the two sides of an account should total the same value. However, in reality, due to statistical discrepancy or imperfections in source data, this is often not the case.

The National Income and Product Account

The National Income and Product Account summarizes total economic activity as the consolidation of the production accounts for all sectors of the economy (business, government, household, and the rest of the world) and business appropriations. It is the account that measures the GDP. The product side of the National Income and Product Account is the sum of personal consumption expenditures, gross private domestic investment, net exports of goods and services, and government purchases of goods and services. The income side is made up of the costs incurred and profits earned in the production of the GNP. On the income side of this account, such items as compensation of employees, proprietors' income, rental income, corporate profits, and net income are totaled to equal national income. National income is then adjusted by the inclusion of business transfer payment, indirect business and tax and nontax liability, and capital consumption allowances, and subsidies are deducted to provide the estimate of GNP. GNP is then adjusted for receipts and payments to and from the rest of the world to produce GDP. Because the underlying source data used in calculating the product side are considered to be more reliable than the data used in calculating the income side, the income side must also be adjusted for statistical discrepancy to make the two sides of the account balance. Therefore, the more accurate product side is designated the official measure of the GDP. The components and structure of the National Income and Product Account are given in Table 5-1.

As noted above, the BEA merges a variety of data to produce the GDP and the NIPAs. A detailed analysis of the principal source data used in preparing the NIPAs reinforces this point. On the income side, data on the compensation of employees alone come from at least seven major sources. Annual tabulations of wages, salaries, and unemployment insurance are provided by the BLS and other relevant agencies, such as the USDA (for farms), the Railroad Retirement Board (for railroad transportation), and the Office of Personnel Management (for federal employees); the Social Security Administration provides data on employer contributions to social insurance; the Internal Revenue Service is the source of information on private pension and profit-sharing funds; and the Health Care Financing Administration provides data on group life and health insurance. On the income side, as an example, sources for

Table 5-1. NIPA Account One: National Income and Product Account

Compensation of employees
  Wages and salaries
    Disbursements
    Wage accruals less disbursements
  Supplements to wages and salaries
    Employers' contributions for
    social insurance
    Other labor income

Proprietors' income with inventory
valuation and capital consumption
adjustments

Rental income of persons with
capital consumption adjustment

Corporate profits with inventory
valuation and capital consumption
adjustments
  Profits before tax
    Profits tax liability
    Profits after tax
      Dividends
      Undistributed profits with
      inventory valuation and capital
      consumption adjustment

Net interest

National income

Business transfer payments
  To persons
  To rest of the world
Indirect business tax and nontax
liability

Less: subsidies less current surplus
of government enterprises

Consumption of fixed capital

Capital consumption allowances

Gross national income

Statistical discrepancy

Gross national product

Less: Receipts of factor income from the
rest of the world

Plus: Payments of factor income to the
rest of the world

Gross domestic product

Personal consumption expenditures
  Durable goods
  Nondurable goods
  Services

Gross private domestic investment
  Fixed investment
    Nonresidential
      Structures
      Producers' durable equipment
    Residential
  Change in business inventories

Net exports of goods and services
  Exports
  Imports

Government purchases
  Federal
    National defense
    Nondefense
  State and local

Gross domestic product

Source: U.S. Bureau of Economic Analysis, *Survey of Current Business* (October 1991), p. 27.

data on government purchases of goods and services include the Office of Management and Budget; the Office of Personnel Management; the Department of Defense; private banks, credit agencies, and investment companies; the Treasury department; the Commodity Credit Corp.; the Census Bureau; and the U.S. Department of Agriculture, all of which supply information on federal defense and nondefense spending. The BLS, the Census Bureau, and the Social Security Administration offer data on state and local compensation; the U.S. Department of Transportation and the Census Bureau supply data on state and local structures; and the Census Bureau provides data on state and local purchases other than compensation and structures.[6]

As previously stated, the National Income and Product Account is the summary account of the NIPA system. It draws on entries from the other four accounts to estimate total national output across all sectors of the economy. The other accounts focus on specific sectors of the economy.

The Personal Income and Outlay Account

The Personal Income and Outlay Account measures personal income from all sources and its disposition. The income side of this account totals personal tax and nontax payments, personal outlays (personal consumption expenditures, interest paid by consumers to business, and personal transfer payments to foreigners), and personal savings, such as personal taxes, outlays, and savings. The product side represents aggregate personal income as the total of wages and salary disbursements, other labor income, proprietors' income, rental income, personal dividend income, personal interest income, and transfer payments to persons (adjusted for contributions for social insurance). Components of this account are given in Table 5-2.

The Government Receipts and Expenditures Account

The Government Receipts and Expenditures Account measures the receipts and expenditures of federal, state, and local governments in the United States. In this account, the income side totaled as government expenditures and surplus. It includes government purchases of goods and services, government transfer payments, net interest paid by government, government subsidies less current surpluses of government enterprises, and government surpluses or deficits, adjusted for dividends received by government and wage accruals less disbursements. The product side summarizes government receipts as the total of personal tax and nontax payments, corporate profits tax liability, indirect business tax and nontax liability, and contributions for social insurance.

Table 5-2. NIPA Account Two: Personal Income and Outlay Account

Personal tax and nontax payments	Wage and salary disbursements
Personal outlays	Other labor income
Personal consumption expenditures	Proprietors' income with inventory
Interest paid by persons	valuation and capital consumption
Personal transfer payments to the	adjustments
rest of the world	Rental income of persons with capital
Personal savings	consumption adjustment
	Personal dividend income
	Dividends
	Less: interest received by
	government
	Personal interest income
	Net interest
	Net interest paid by government
	Interest paid by persons
	Transfer payments to persons
	From business
	From government
	Less: personal contributions for
	social insurance
Personal taxes, outlays, and savings	**Personal income**

Source: U.S. Bureau of Economic Analysis, *Survey of Current Business* (October 1991), p. 27.

Table 5-3 outlines the structure of the Government Receipts and Expenditures Account.

The Foreign Transactions Account

The Foreign Transactions Account is a summary of income and output to and from foreign sources. The income side is the aggregate of receipts from the rest of the world. It is composed of exports of goods and services, receipts of factor income, and capital grants received by the United States. The product side is the total of payments to the rest of the world, including imports of goods and services, payments of factor income, transfer payments to the rest of the world, and net foreign investment. Table 5-4 presents the components of this account.

The Gross Savings and Investment Account

The Gross Savings and Investment Account covers all sectors of the economy (business, government, personal, etc.) and measures savings and investment. The income side of this account represents gross investment

Table 5-3. NIPA Account Three: Government Receipts and
Expenditures Account

Purchases	Personal tax and nontax payments
Transfer payments	Corporate profits tax liability
To persons	Indirect business tax and nontax
To rest of the world	liability
Net interest paid	Contributions for social insurance
Less: dividends received by	Employer
government	Personal
Subsidies less current surplus	
of government enterprises	
Less: wage accruals less disbursements	
Surplus or deficit (—), national income	
and product accounts	
Federal	
State and local	
Government expenditures and surplus	**Government receipts**

Source: U.S. Bureau of Economic Analysis, *Survey of Current Business* (October 1991), p. 28

Table 5-4. NIPA Account Four: Foreign Transactions Account

Exports of goods and services	Imports of goods and services
Receipts of factor income	Payments of factor income
Capital grants received by	Transfer payments to rest of the world (net)
the United States	From persons (net)
	From government (net)
	From business
	Net foreign investment
Receipts from rest of the world	**Payments to rest of the world**

Source: U.S. Bureau of Economic Analysis, *Survey of Current Business* (October 1991), p. 28.

as the total of gross private domestic investment and net foreign investment. The product side aggregates gross saving as the total of personal savings, wage accruals (less disbursements), undistributed corporate profits, consumption of fixed government surplus (or deficit), and capital grants received by the United States adjusted for statistical discrepancy.[7] Components of this account are given in Table 5-5.

Publication of the GDP

GDP figures are initially released to the public in the form of a press release. Immediately following the press release, the same summary data are published in *BEA Report*. The official publication of GDP estimates is in the monthly *Survey of Current Business*. Following a brief overview of current economic conditions in "The Business Situation," *Survey*

Table 5-5. NIPA Account Five: Gross Savings and Investment Account

Gross private domestic investment	Personal savings
Net foreign investment	Wage accruals less disbursements
	Undistributed corporate profits with inventory valuation and capital consumption adjustments
	Government surplus or deficit (−), national income and product accounts
	Capital grants received by the U.S. (net)
	Statistical discrepancy
Gross Investment	**Gross saving and statistical discrepancy**

Source: U.S. Bureau of Economic Analysis, *Survey of Current Business* (October 1991), p. 28.

generally provides data for the NIPAs for the most recent three years. Revised estimates for recent years are also published annually in the July issue. In addition to the five summary accounts presented here as Tables 5-1 through 5-5, there are a variety of more detailed and specialized tables, including tables grouped under the following thematic headings: Product and Income, Personal Income and Outlays, and Employment by Industry; Fixed-Weighted Price Indexes and Implicit Price Deflators; Supplementary Tables; and Seasonally Unadjusted Estimates.

The *Survey of Current Business* provides a variety of important background information on the NIPAs, including methodology, analysis of revisions, a recurring "Index to Items Appearing in the National Income and Product Account Tables," and background on source data for specific entries in the accounts. It also has two supplements that provide historical data and background information for the GNP. *Business Statistics*, a biennial, includes historic data for the GNP and other components of the NIPAs for approximately twenty years. It also includes methodological notes and references to sources of additional information. The supplement *National Income and Products Accounts: Statistical Tables* appears approximately every five years. This publication gives data for the most recent benchmark revision of the NIPAs. It also outlines the definitions and classifications that underlie the NIPA system.

Other Measures of Production

Index of Industrial Production

The Federal Reserve Board of Governors is responsible for another major measure of production, the Index of Industrial Production. The Federal

Reserve is the nation's central bank, and as part of its charge to make and administer national banking and monetary policy, it produces relevant statistical data. The Index of Industrial Production differs from both GNP and the GDP in several respects. At the simplest level, the Federal Reserve measure differs from the NIPAs because it is expressed as an index, rather than as a measure of actual output. In addition, the Index of Industrial Production monitors production for only selected industries, where the GNP and GDP attempt to gauge total output; the Federal Reserve index also covers only 265 mining and manufacturing industries that equate to approximately one-third of the total GNP.[8] A further difference arises in the breadth of production activities included in the index. Where the GDP/GNP reflects only the value of final sale goods and services, the Index of Industrial Production includes intermediate and final products. Furthermore, the Federal Reserve statistics measure change in physical volume or quantity of output, not value, as with the GNP and GDP.[9]

Publication

The Index of Industrial Production is calculated monthly and announced in a Federal Reserve *Statistical Release*. Figures are later reported in *Federal Reserve Bulletin*. As with the price indexes outlined in chapter 4, the Index of Industrial Production is not a single index, but a family of indexes, and in addition to the aggregate index, measures are calculated by product type for final products, consumer goods, equipment, intermediate products and for materials (durable, nondurable, and energy materials).

Input-Output Accounts

The U.S. input-output accounts are another important measure of industrial production. Input-output tables are closely related to the NIPAs. However, instead of focusing on production in terms of the value of final sales of goods and services, the input-output accounts use the same data to measure the basic relationships between industries by examining the movement of commodities between industries throughout the production process.[10] The most recent benchmark input-output tables for the United States cover the year 1977 and are based on the detailed industry statistics collected in that year by the Bureau of the Census as part of the economic censuses.

The input-output tables, produced by the BEA, examine input-output relationships between eighty-five industries and commodities (based on SIC categories). These categories are given in Table 5-6. As shown in that table, the 85-industry level allows for some specificity in identifying industries. Coal mining; radio, TV, and communications

Table 5-6. Industry Coverage in 85-Industry Input-Output Table, 1983

Industry no. and Industry	Industry no. and Industry
1 Livestock and livestock products	44 Farm and garden machinery
2 Other agricultural products	45 Construction and mining machinery
3 Forestry and fishery products	46 Materials handling machinery and equipment
4 Agricultural, forestry and fishery services	47 Metalworking machinery and equipment
5 Iron and ferro-alloy ores mining	48 Special industry machinery and equipment
6 Non-ferrous metal ores mining	49 General industrial machinery and equipment
7 Coal mining	50 Miscellaneous machinery except electrical
8 Crude petroleum and natural gas	51 Office computing and accounting machinery
9 Stone and clay mining and quarrying	52 Service industry machines
10 Chemical and fertilizer mining	53 Electric industrial equipment and apparatus
11 New construction	54 Household appliances
12 Repair and maintenance construction	55 Electric lighting and wiring equipment
13 Ordinance and accessories	56 Radio, TV, and communication equipment
14 Food and kindred products	57 Electronic components and accessories
15 Tobacco manufactures	58 Miscellaneous electrical machinery and supplies
16 Broad and narrow fabrics, yarns and thread mills	59 Motor vehicles and equipment
17 Miscellaneous textile goods and floor coverings	60 Aircraft and parts
18 Apparel	61 Other transportation equipment
19 Miscellaneous fabricated textile products	62 Scientific and controlling equipment
20 Lumber and wood products except containers	63 Optical, ophthalmic and photographic equipment
21 Wood containers	64 Miscellaneous manufacturing
22 Household furniture	65 Transportation and warehousing
23 Other furniture and fixtures	66 Communications, except radio and TV
24 Paper and allied products except containers	67 Radio and TV broadcasting
25 Paperboard containers and boxes	68 Private electric, gas, water, and sanitary services
26 Printing and publishers	69 Wholesale and retail trade
27 Chemicals and selected chemical products	70 Finance and insurance
28 Plastics and synthetic materials	71 Real estate and rental
29 Drugs, cleaning and toilet preparations	72 Hotels, personal and repair services (exc. auto)
30 Paints and allied products	73 Business services
31 Petroleum refining and related industries	74 Eating and drinking establishments
32 Rubber and miscellaneous plastic products	75 Automobile repair and services
33 Leather tanning and finishing	76 Amusements
34 Footwear and other leather products	77 Health, educational, and social services and nonprofit organizations
35 Glass and glass products	78 Federal government enterprises
36 Stone and clay products	79 State and local government enterprises
37 Primary iron and steel manufacturing	81 Scrap and used goods
38 Primary nonferrous metals manufacturing	82 Government industry
39 Metal containers	83 Rest of the world industry
40 Heating, plumbing, and fabricated structural metal products	84 Household industry
41 Screw machine products and stampings	85 Inventory valuation adjustment
42 Other fabricated metal products	
43 Engines and turbines	

Source: U.S. Bureau of Economic Analysis, *Survey of Current Business* (February 1989), p. 30–36.

equipment; and finance and insurance all are assigned unique numbers in the scheme.

There are five tables in the U.S. input-output accounts. These tables provide detailed information on the value of each commodity used by each industry, the value of each commodity produced by each industry, the direct and indirect effects of final demand on commodity output, and the direct and indirect effects of final demand on industry output. Annual updates that are definitionally consistent with the 1977 benchmark are also produced. However, for these annual updates, only two of the five input-output tables are widely disseminated. Tables 5-7 and 5-8 provide data from the 1983 make table. In Table 5-7, entries in a row show the distribution of commodities produced by the industry identified at the top of the column. In Table 5-8, columns show the distribution of industries producing the commodity identified at the beginning of each row. In these tables, all entries represent value in millions of dollars at producers' prices.

Publication

The benchmark input-output tables are released as monographs by the BEA. The annual accounts appear in *Survey of Current Business*. However, as stated above, only the use and make tables appear in printed form. The remaining three tables are available directly from the BEA in machine-readable form only. There is a lag of several years in the production of the annual accounts; the 1983 accounts were published in February of 1989.

Caveats and Limitations

In the past, GNP and the NIPAs have generally been credited as accurate and adequate measures of the economic activity they attempt to quantify. However, the quality of the accounts is a function of both the quality of the source data and the conceptual adequacy of the accounting system. There have been instances of potentially dangerous inaccuracies in the estimates. In addition, the NIPAs' coverage of certain sectors of the economy is problematic. The accuracy of GNP estimates has sometimes been subject to question; however, when the early flash estimate of the GNP was dropped, the move was criticized as a loss of early, though rough, data.

The general concensus among critics is that the GNP understates economic activity. The GNP and the NIPAs have had difficulty measuring the underground economy. Some outside estimates of the size of the underground economy run as high as 33 percent of the U.S. GDP.[11] Non-farm proprietors' income (i.e., personal income from self-employment) is underreported to the IRS (the source for much of the BEA's personal

Table 5-7. The Make of Commodities by Industry, 1983: Distribution of Industries Producing Specific Commodities

Industry no.	Commodity no.	1-13	14	15	16	17	18	19	20	21
24	Paper and allied products except containers		*	41	3	199		56	119	
25	Paperboard containers and boxes					4			3	1
26	Printing and publishing			4		40		12	13	

Industry no.	Commodity no.	22	23	24	25	26	27	28	29	30
24	Paper and allied products except containers		2	60,353	92	368	296	34	18	6
25	Paperboard containers and boxes			117	19,763	49				
26	Printing and publishing		15	521	72	57,893	6			

Industry no.	Commodity no.	31	32	33	34	35	36	37-38	39	40
24	Paper and allied products except containers	4	400				32			
25	Paperboard containers and boxes		200		3				15	
26	Printing and publishing		39		5	19			15	13

Industry no.	Commodity no.	41	42	43	44-45	46	47	48	49	50
24	Paper and allied products except containers		167					43	8	
25	Paperboard containers and boxes		20	29		12	2	2		
26	Printing and publishing			88			12	28		1

Industry no.	Commodity no.	51	52	53	54	55	56	57	58	59
24	Paper and allied products except containers	259		2		2	9	248	6	13
25	Paperboard containers and boxes									
26	Printing and publishing	79					27			

Industry no	Commodity no.	60-61	62	63	64	65-72	73	74-79	81	82-85
24	Paper and allied products except containers		52	69	163		13		5	
25	Paperboard containers and boxes				*		37		*	
26	Printing and publishing		13	28	111		34,796		26	

Source: U.S. Bureau of Economic Analysis, *Survey of Current Business* (February 1989), p. 30–36.

Note: This table provides information on the distribution of industries producing the three commodities given as examples. The double lines between cells indicate industries for which there was no production of the commodities used in this example.

* less than $500,000

Table 5-8. The Make of Commodities by Industry, 1983: Distribution of Commodities Produced by Specific Industries

Industry no.	Paper and allied products except containers (24)	Paperboard containers and boxes (25)	Printing and publishing (26)
1-13			
14	56	14	12
15	5		
16	101		14
17	57		14
18	16		
19	62	1	16
20	120	10	*
21	10	3	
22	6		
23	9		6
24	60,353	92	368
25	117	19,763	49
26	521	72	57,893
27	114		61
28	6		
29	15		5
30	1		
31	21	6	
32	220	35	42
33			
34	4		5
35		10	4
36	108		*
37	7	8	7
38	27		
39	10	83	212
40	15		2
41	3	22	2
42	236	92	81
43			
44		13	
45			
46			*
47	2	2	8
48	4		
49			
50	1		
51	23		53
52		3	
53	8		1
54	17		
55	16		11
56	4		11
57	13		*
58			
59	40		
60			27
61		1	
62	57		4
63	76		31
64	71	4	75
65-85			
Total	62,549	20,232	59,011

Source: U.S. Bureau of Economic Analysis, *Survey of Current Business* (February 1989), p. 30–36.
Note: This table provides information on the distribution of products produced by the three industries given as examples. The double lines between cells indicate products for which there was no production by the industries used in this example.
* less than $500,000

income data) by as much as 60 percent.[12] Until the recent introduction of an index of change in computer prices, the GNP also understated production because it assumed constant prices for computer equipment when, in fact, prices for the period 1972–1984 dropped an average of 14 percent per year.[13]

A private consultant to the Joint Economic Committee has commented, "Although the reliability of the GNP estimates generally has been quite good, there have been occasions during the past decade when inaccuracies in the early quarterly estimates have made it difficult for policymakers to make informed policy decisions."[14] Figures for business inventory and fixed investment are frequently the source of inaccuracy in GNP estimates. In what the BEA characterizes as its biggest failure, a buildup in business inventories in 1973 to 1974 was drastically underestimated, and this delayed identification of the onset of a recession.[15] In another problem area, for the period 1977 to 1979, business fixed investment was revised upward from 8 to 10 percent due to problems with the source data.[16] Certainly, the BEA's estimates of the GNP can be no better than the source data from which they are calculated. In a system where figures are reported from so many sources, and there is so little opportunity to monitor quality or tailor methodology employed by other sources for the purposes of the NIPAs, there is room for such errors to occur.

There has been debate over the BEA's decision to stop calculating flash estimates of the GNP. For the period 1983 to 1985, the BEA published an estimate of the GNP for the quarter in the final weeks before the quarter ended. Generally, the discrepancy between the flash and the later preliminary estimate was large. When the BEA announced in early 1986 that it would no longer calculate the flash estimate, its chief economist was quoted as saying that one reason for the flash's demise was that "the public was coming to regard it as a legitimate statistic."[17] Others have also argued that earlier figures for a given period are always less accurate than later estimates and that the flash provided a valuable, though rough, early look at economic activity. However, in an article in *The Wall Street Journal*, Stephen K. McNees, vice president of the Federal Reserve Bank of Boston, commented that "three studies [have shown that] . . . the 'flash' estimates of nominal and real GNP have been at least as reliable as the subsequent preliminary estimate. The 'flash' is probably more useful for economic decision making because it is available earlier."[18] Economist Courtney Slater has pointed out in testimony before the Joint Economic Committee that "the Bureau of Economic Analysis can make the best forecast of the current quarter that can be made because they are closer to the data that is coming in than anybody else. What we are going to have now is a bunch of other people running around making forecasts that won't be as good."[19]

Notes

1. U.S. Bureau of the Census, *Statistical Abstract of the United States* (Washington, D.C.: U.S. Government Printing Office, 1987), p.403.
2. U.S. Bureau of Economic Analysis, *National Income and Product Accounts of the United States, 1929–1982: Statistical Tables* (Washington, D.C.: U.S. Government Printing Office, September 1986), p.ix.
3. John Walmsley, *Dictionary of International Finance*, (Westport, Conn.: Greenwood, 1979), p.127.
4. U.S. Bureau of Economic Analysis, *Survey of Current Business*, February 1988, p.4.
5. U.S. Bureau of Economic Analysis, *An Introduction of National Income Accounting, Methodology Paper Series MP-1* (Washington, D.C.: U.S. Government Printing Office), p.1–2.
6. U.S. Bureau of Economic Analysis, "The U.S. National Income and Product Accounts: Revised Estimates—Methodology," *Survey of Current Business*, July 1990, p.19–33.
7. Ibid., p.36–37.
8. Carol S. Carson, "Gross National Product and Related Measures," in *The Handbook of Economic and Financial Measures*, ed. Frank N. Fabozzi and Harry I. Greenfield (Homewood, Ill.: Dow Jones-Irwin, 1984), p.36.
9. *The New Palgrave: A Dictionary of Economics* (London: Macmillan Press, 1987), p.860.
10. U.S. Bureau of Economic Analysis, *Detailed Input-output Structure of the U.S. Economy, 1977* (Washington, D.C.: U.S. Government Printing Office, 1984).
11. "The Shadow Economy: Grossly Deceptive Product," *The Economist*, September 19, 1987, p.25–28.
12. U.S. Congress, Joint Economic Committee, *The Quality of the Nation's Economic Statistics: Hearing, March 17–April 17, 1986* (Washington, D.C.: U.S. Government Printing Office, 1986), p.45–46.
13. Ibid., p. 46–47.
14. U.S. Congress, Joint Economic Committee, *Maintaining the Quality of Economic Data* (97th Congress, 1st Session, Joint Committee Print) (Washington, D.C.: U.S. Government Printing Office, 1981), p.1.
15. U.S. Bureau of Economic Analysis, *The Use of National Income and Product Accounts for Public Policy: Our Successes and Failures*, Bureau of Economic Analysis Statistical Paper 43 (Washington, D.C.: U.S. Government Printing Office, January 1986), p.10.
16. U.S. Congress, Joint Economic Committee, *Maintaining the Quality of Economic Data*, p.10–11.
17. "Not So Sad Passing of an Economic Indicator," *Business Week*, February 10, 1986, p.30.
18. Stephen McNees, "GNP 'Flash' Gives Good Picture," *The Wall Street Journal*, February 27, 1986, p.25.
19. U.S. Congress, Joint Economic Committee, *The Quality of the Nation's Economic Statistics*, p.95.

Bibliography

"Answers That Unveil the Underground Economy." *Business Week* (October 11, 1982), p.14.

Board of Governors Federal Reserve. *Federal Reserve Bulletin*, monthly.

———. *Statistical Release*, irregular.

Carson, Carol S. "Gross National Product and Related Measures." In *The Handbook of Economic and Financial Measures*, p.3–39. Ed. Frank N. Fabozzi and Harry I. Greenfield. Homewood, Ill.: Dow Jones-Irwin, 1984.

———. "The Underground Economy: An Introduction." *Survey of Current Business* (May 1984), p.21–37.

Frey, Bruno S., and others. "The Hidden Economy: State and Prospects for Measurement." *Review of Economics and Statistics Series 30* (March 1984), p.1–23.

Hosley, Joan D., and others. "A Revision of the Index of Industrial Production." *Federal Reserve Bulletin* (July 1985), p.487–97.

Lee, Susan. "The Unmeasurable Economy." *Forbes* (June 3, 1985), p.99–102.

McNees, Stephen. "GNP 'Flash' Gives Good Picture." *The Wall Street Journal* (February 27, 1986), p.25.

The New Palgrave: A Dictionary of Economics. London: Macmillan Press, 1987.

"Not So Sad Passing of an Economic Indicator." *Business Week* (February 10, 1986), p.30.

Parker, Robert B. "Why Economic Indicators Often Go Wrong." *Business Week* (October 17, 1983), p.168–69.

Rogers, Mark R. "Tracking the Economy: Fundamentals for Understanding Data." *Federal Reserve Bank of Atlanta Economic Review* (March/April 1989), p.30–48.

Ross, Irwin. "Why the Underground Economy Is Booming." *Fortune* (October 9, 1978), p.92–99.

"The Shadow Economy: Grossly Deceptive Product." *The Economist* (September 19, 1987), p.25–28.

"The Underground Economy." *U.S. News and World Report* (October 22, 1979), p.49–52.

"The Underground Economy's Hidden Force." *Business Week* (April 5, 1982), p.64–70.

U.S. Bureau of Economic Analysis. *BEA Reports: Gross National Product*. Springfield, Va.: National Technical Information Service, monthly.

———. *Business Statistics*. Washington, D.C.: U.S. Government Printing Office, biennially.

———. *Detailed Input-output Structure of the U.S. Economy, 1977*. 2 v. Washington, D.C.: U.S. Government Printing Office, 1984.

———. *An Introduction to National Income Accounting. Methodology Paper Series MP-1*. Washington, D.C.: U.S. Government Printing Office, March 1985.

———. *National Income and Product Accounts of the United States, 1929–1982: Statistical Tables*. Washington, D.C.: U.S. Government Printing Office, quinquennially.

———. *Readings in Concepts and Methods of National Income Statistics*. Springfield, Va.: National Technical Information Service, 1976.

———. *Sources of Error in Input-output Tables of the U.S. Economy: 1968, 1969 and 1970.* Bureau of Economic Analysis Staff Paper No. 31. Springfield, Va.: National Technical Information Service, 1975.

————. *Survey of Current Business.* Washington, D.C.: U.S. Government Printing Office, monthly.

————. *The Use of National Income and Product Accounts for Public Policy: Our Successes and Failures.* Bureau of Economic Analysis Statistical Paper 43. Washington, D.C.: U.S. Government Printing Office, January 1986.

————. *A User's Guide to BEA Information.* Washington, D.C.: U.S. Government Printing Office, irregular.

U.S. Bureau of the Census. *Statistical Abstract of the United States.* Washington, D.C.: U.S. Government Printing Office, annually.

U.S. Congress. Joint Economic Committee. *The Quality of the Nation's Economic Statistics: Hearing, March 17–April 17, 1986.* Washington, D.C.: U.S. Government Printing Office, 1986.

————. *Maintaining the Quality of Economic Data.* 97th Congress, 1st Session, Joint Committee Print. Washington, D.C.: U.S. Government Printing Office, 1981.

————. *1980 Supplement to Economic Indicators: Historical and Descriptive Background.* Washington, D.C.: U.S. Government Printing Office, 1980, p.1–19.

Walmsley, John. *Dictionary of International Finance.* Westport, Conn.: Greenwood Press, 1979, p.127.

Young, Allan H. "Alternative Measures of Real GNP." *Survey of Current Business* (April 1989), p.27–34.

6   Foreign Trade

In recent years, the balance of trade has come to the forefront as a perceived indicator of national economic well-being. A positive balance of trade is viewed as one indication of a healthy economy; a high level of exports indicates high levels of employment. Conversely, a trade deficit can be viewed negatively for a variety of reasons—especially because a trade deficit must be financed by debts incurred to foreigners and implies a high dependence on foreign economies. The U.S. government has collected data on its trade with other countries since 1790, when the Secretary of the Treasury estimated annual import and export values. Today, U.S. foreign trade is tracked in great detail. Since 1941, the Bureau of the Census has been responsible for the compilation of U.S. merchandise import and export data. These data are an important analytical tool for evaluating economic trends, as well as the impact of public policy and international trade agreements such as the General Agreement on Tariffs and Trade. In addition, the BEA publishes comprehensive data on international economic transactions.

Foreign trade statistics are among the most detailed statistical series compiled by the U.S. government. There are several methodologies for determining the value of imports and exports. The three most common methods in the United States are F.A.S. (or free alongside ship), C.I.F. (or cost, insurance, and freight), and customs value. In addition, there are several detailed schemes for classifying import and export product categories. The Census Bureau uses its Schedule E for exports and Schedule A for imports. Census Bureau trade figures generally cover merchandise only; those produced by the BEA include services and other international transactions. An understanding and awareness of these schemes and their differences is essential to informed use of foreign trade statistics.

Merchandise Trade Data

The Census Bureau is responsible for the compilation of current statistics on U.S. foreign trade, including imports, exports, and shipping. The Census Bureau's foreign trade data track the physical movement of merchandise in and out of U.S. customs areas (the fifty states, the District of Columbia, and Puerto Rico). Separate data series and definitions are employed for exports and imports.

Export series cover the movement of merchandise from the United States to foreign countries. Some types of shipments are excluded: shipments to U.S. armed forces and diplomatic missions, supplies and equipment (including fuel) for vessels engaged in foreign trade, monetary gold and issued coins, and household and personal effects of travelers. Various series track exports of domestic and foreign merchandise (re-exports). "Domestic merchandise" is defined as commodities grown, produced, or manufactured in the United States, or changed or enhanced by further manufacture in the United States. "Foreign merchandise" is defined as merchandise of foreign origin entered into U.S. customs as imports that, at the time of re-export, is substantially unchanged. While it might seem that little imported merchandise is re-exported, this is not the case. For example, for the period January to June 1988, 468,388 gallons of U.S.-produced ice cream (valued at $961,000) were exported to Hong Kong. In addition, during the same period, 16,592 gallons of foreign-produced ice cream (valued at $33,000) were exported from the United States to Hong Kong. The amount of re-exported ice cream to Hong Kong represents approximately 3.3 percent of total exports for the period.

Import series cover total arrivals of merchandise, except in-transit shipments. Certain types of import shipments are excluded from the data series: government imports, monetary gold and issued coins, and items of small importance. Both export and import series provide data on merchandise trade volume and value. In-transit shipments would be imports that are really destined for other countries and enter the United States only in transit to other locations. For example, merchandise shipped by truck from Mexico and destined for Canada must enter the United States in transit to its final destination. Imports are also broken down into two broad categories: general imports and imports for consumption. General imports reflect total arrivals, whether or not merchandise enters into consumption channels. That is, some general imports clear customs and are immediately released for consumption in U.S. markets.

Other general imports do not immediately clear customs, but are held in customs-bonded warehouses for a period of time before they are either re-exported or released for consumption in U.S. markets. Imports for consumption are only those imports entered into U.S. consumption channels. While it might seem that re-exports account for an inconsequential percentage of total exports, the June 1988 issue of *FT135: U.S. General Imports and Imports for Consumption* reported that the customs value of general imports for the period January to June 1988 was $215,848,689. For the same period, the customs valuation of imports for consumption was $213,974,711. By inference, some $1,873,978 (or nearly 1 percent) of imports did not enter U.S. consumption channels. [1]

Commodity Classification and Valuation

As stated above, nomenclature and valuation methodology are important concepts in the reporting of import and export data. In this context, nomenclature is the system of definitions and categories used to classify disaggregated trade data into product groups. When goods cross the U.S. border, they are assigned a seven-digit product code, according to one of two nomenclatures (one for imports, one for exports). To allow for various types of analysis and comparison, these codes are aggregated into broader categories. These systems are based on international standards that facilitate cross-national comparisons. In the 1950s, the United Nations developed the Standard International Trade Classification (SITC), a standard still in use today. A new international system, the Harmonized Commodity Description and Coding System, is now being phased into use. [2]

The Census Bureau uses several commodity classification systems. For imports, the Tariff Schedule of the U.S. Annotated (TSUSA) provides 10,500 seven-digit commodity classifications and is the nomenclature by which imports are originally recorded. Schedule A is an SITC-based rearrangement of TSUSA. For exports, Schedule B provides 4,500 seven-digit commodity classes and is the nomenclature by which exports are originally recorded. Schedule E is the SITC-based rearrangement of Schedule B. [3] Trade nomenclatures are hierarchical schemes in which nested numeric codes are assigned to product categories.

Table 6-1 shows a sample of the groupings of import and export categories. This sample notes the tree-like structure of the schedules, providing varying levels of aggregation machinery and transport equipment and parts. In the information provided, the Schedule A imports commodity categories. The Schedule E export commodity categories are largely comparable.

As with nomenclature, several systems are available for placing a monetary value on imported or exported goods. For example, in recent

Table 6-1. Select Schedule A Groupings of Commodities for Machinery and Transport Equipment

Schedule A classes	Commodity groupings
7	Machinery and transport equipment
71	Power-generating machinery and equipment
72	Machinery specialized for particular industries
73	Metal-working machinery
74	General industrial machinery and equipment, NSPF* and parts thereof, NSPF*
75	Office machines and automatic data processing equipment
751	Office machines
751.1	Typewriters, except typewriters incorporating a calculating mechanism
751.2	Calculators, adding machines, cash registers, and other office machines incorporating a calculating mechanism
751.8	Office machines, NSPF*
76	Telecommunications, sound recordings, reproducing apparatus, and equipment
77	Electrical machinery, apparatus, and appliances, NSPF*, and electrical parts thereof
78	Road vehicles
79	Other transport equipment

Sources: U.S. Bureau of the Census, *FT135: General Imports and Imports for Consumption-Schedule A Commodity by Country* (Washington, D.C.: U.S. Government Printing Office, June 1988) and U.S. Bureau of the Census, *FT410: U.S. Exports—Schedule E Commodity by Country* (Washington, D.C.: U.S. Government Printing Office, May 1988).

* NSPF = Not specifically provided for

years, the federal government has employed three different valuation methodologies for traded goods. For imports, both C.I.F. and customs valuation are available. The C.I.F. valuation basis is the more inclusive measure; it values imports at the first port of entry and includes customs value plus freight, insurance, and charges other than import duties. The customs valuation basis values imports as appraised by the Customs Service; import duties, freight, insurance, and other charges are excluded. For exports, the F.A.S. export valuation basis is used. F.A.S. values U.S. exports at the port of export, including transaction price, freight, and insurance costs incurred in placing merchandise at the U.S. port of export. [4]

While foreign trade data are compiled by the Census Bureau, data are largely collected by the Customs Bureau. Export data are based on information from the customs declaration forms filed by shippers. In addition to using the customs forms, the Census Bureau collects some data directly from exporters. For imports, data are collected from a variety of formal entry forms, as well as directly from select import brokers.

Publication

The Census Bureau provides monthly and annual figures for foreign trade. These data are officially published in the various FT (or Foreign Trade) series. Summary data first appear one to two months after the period of coverage. *FT900: Summary of U.S. Export and Import Merchandise Trade* provides an overview of U.S. foreign trade. Each month, *FT900* presents data for a five-month period. The publication generally consists of eight tables. One covers the overall trade balance for the most current month of coverage and the year to date. The remaining tables provide data on the volume and value of U.S. imports and exports by countries and regions according to several different nomenclatures and valuation methods. In *FT900*, trade is broken down into various product categories at the one-digit level only. The publication *FT990: Highlights of U.S. Export and Import Trade* generally appears two to three months after the period of coverage. *FT990* provides data on the balance of trade and on the volume and value of U.S. imports and exports. Summary historic data cover the previous and current year only. Data are provided as seasonally adjusted and unadjusted; several schedules are employed. Detailed monthly data for exports appear in *FT410: U.S. Exports—Schedule E Commodity by Country*. This publication presents three lengthy tables on the volume and value of U.S. exports of domestic and foreign merchandise. Commodity codes provide detail from the one- to the four-digit level. All data are for the current month and year to date.

Monthly import data appear in *FT135: U.S. General Imports and Imports for Consumption—Schedule A Commodity by Country*. This publication generally provides two lengthy tables on the quantity and value of U.S. inputs for some three thousand commodity groups by country of origin. Data are broken down to the seven-digit level only, and are provided for the current month and year to date. As this volume was being compiled, the Census Bureau was in the process of moving the distribution of its foreign trade data, at least in part, to CD-ROM format. The exact impact on its print or microfiche publication series was unclear.

Table two from *FT410*, "Schedule E Commodity by Country—Domestic Merchandise," provides data on the net quantity (in the unit specified for each commodity) and total value (in thousands of U.S. dollars) of exports of domestic merchandise by country. A sample of data from table two is provided here as Table 6-2.

Table 6-3 provides data for select import commodities by country of origin from table two in *FT135*. Both customs and C.I.F. value are provided, as well as data on the net quantity of imports.

Monthly data appearing in the FT series are cumulated in several annual series. The annual *U.S. Foreign Trade Highlights* provides approxi-

Table 6-2. Schedule E Exports Commodity by Country, Domestic Merchandise for Classification Number 7511020 "Typewriters, Portable, Non-Calculating, Non-Automatic"—May 1988

Country of destination	Current month		Cumulative, January to date	
	Net quantity	Value (000 dollars)	Net quantity	Value (000 dollars)
7511020: Typewriters, portable, noncalculating, non-automatic, no.				
Canada	30	11	412	73
Mexico	100	4	507	40
Guatamal	—	—	1,126	70
Salvadr	100	7	1,881	128
Panama	—	—	1,500	66
Venez	677	55	1,298	98
Brazil	274	19	314	28
U King	—	—	100	38
France	—	—	188	49
FRGerm	—	—	690	113
Italy	10	4	66	26
Phil R	164	11	568	43
HGKong	700	49	700	49
OthCty*	272	72	1,663	272
Total	2,327	233	11,013	1,091

Source: U.S. Bureau of the Census, *FT410: U.S. Exports—Schedule E Commodity by Country* (May 1988), p. 2–307.

— represents zero
* means other countries

mately 50 tables and analysis. Several other series generally appear about six months after the year of coverage in the bureau's FT series. Key annual publications are provided in Table 6-4.

International Transactions Data

The BEA collects and disseminates data on U.S. international transactions, or the balance of payments. These data are more comprehensive than the Census Bureau's merchandise trade data. In addition to merchandise trade, the U.S. balance of payments includes all other U.S. transactions with foreigners, such as service transactions, foreign aid, interest payments, and other forms of investment. The Foreign Transactions Account of the NIPAs is the summary record of these transactions. The International Transactions Account provides a detailed record of the balance of payments and is composed of exports of goods, services, and income; imports of goods, services, and income; unilateral transfers; U.S. assets abroad (net increase and outflow); and foreign assets in the United States (net increase and outflow).

Table 6-3. Schedule A Imports Commodity by Country for Classification Number 7512110 "Electronic Calculators, Hand Held or Pocket Type"—June 1988

Country of origin	Current month, general imports			Cumulative, January to date, general imports			Cumulative, January to date, imports for consumption	
	Net quantity	Value (thousands ___ of dollars) ___		Net quantity	Value (thousands ___ of dollars) ___		Net quantity	Customs value*
		Customs	C.i.f.		Customs	C.i.f.		
7512110: Electronic calculators, hand held or pocket type, no.								
Sweden	43	2	2	722	37	38	722	37
Switzld	37,000	53	55	38,162	61	63	38,162	61
Italy	102,751	802	818	596,169	4,835	4,962	596,169	4,835
Singarp	90	24	27	701	42	46	201	26
China M	378,440	757	792	1,754,402	2,820	2,932	1,721,652	2,762
Kor Rep	6,000	13	13	646,361	2,236	2,274	646,361	2,236
HGKong	1,408,262	3,345	3,442	7,120,157	20,096	20,673	7,117,647	19,925
China T	1,170,530	4,968	5,072	6,731,133	25,453	26,093	6,732,832	25,469
Japan	448,118	3,127	3,224	1,828,439	13,223	13,461	1,738,779	12,234
Ivy Cst	—	—	—	15,120	104	105	15,120	104
OthCty**	3,613	12	13	32,927	104	108	20,456	86
Total	3,554,847	13,103	13,459	18,764,293	69,011	70,755	18,628,101	67,774

Source: U.S. Bureau of the Census, *FT135: U.S. General Imports and Imports for Consumption* (June 1988), p. 2–214.

* thousands of dollars
** other countries
— represents zero

The Foreign Transactions Account

As mentioned above, the summary statement of the balance of payments is the Foreign Transactions Account. The Foreign Transactions Account is part of the NIPAs, which are discussed in detail in chapter 5. The NIPAs are designed to measure total national output or production across all sectors of the economy. In the NIPAs, there are four basic sectors for

Table 6-4. Key Annual FT Series

Series	Title
FT446	U.S. Exports—Schedule B Commodity by Country
FT450	U.S. Exports—Schedule E Commodity Groupings by World Area
FT455	U.S. Exports—World Area by Schedule E Commodity Grouping
FT150	U.S. General Imports—Commodity Groupings by World Region
FT246	U.S. Imports for Consumption and General Imports: TSUSA Commodity by Country of Origin
FT155	U.S. General Imports and Exports—World Area and Country of Origin by Schedule A Commodity Groupings

Table 6-5. NIPA Account Four: Foreign Transactions Account

Exports of goods and services	Imports of goods and services
Receipts of factor income	Payments of factor income
Capital grants received by the United States	Transfer payments to rest of the world (net)
	From persons (net)
	From government (net)
	From business
	Net foreign investment
Receipts from the rest of the world	**Payments to the rest of the world**

Source: U.S. Bureau of Economic Analysis, *Survey of Current Business* (October 1991), p. 28.

which economic transactions are recorded. They are business, household, government, and the rest of the world. The Foreign Transactions Account records the exchange of U.S. goods, services, and financial assets with the rest of the world.[5] As with the other accounts in the NIPAs, the Foreign Transactions Account employs a double-entry bookkeeping system. Because each transaction involves the exchange of one good, service, or financial asset for another, it is represented in the account by two theoretically offsetting entries. The income side of the account is receipts from the rest of the world. The product side is payments to the rest of the world.

Table 6-5 presents a summary of the Foreign Transactions Account. In addition to this summary table, the account provides specialized information on such topics as constant dollar exports and imports and trade by end-use category.

Publication

The Foreign Transactions Account is published, along with the rest of the NIPAs, on a quarterly basis in *Survey of Current Business. National Income and Product Accounts: Statistical Tables* provides the most recent benchmark revisions for the account and is produced approximately every five years.

The International Transactions Account

The BEA also collects and disseminates detailed data on the balance of payments. These data are published as the International Transactions Account. The International Transactions Account actually provides the basis for calculating the more condensed Foreign Transactions Account; however, the International Transactions Account is calculated on a different accounting basis. Therefore, there are a few definitional and statistical differences between the two accounts. The International Transactions Account provides data on economic transactions between residents of the United States and residents of the rest of the world. All reported, recorded, and estimated foreign transactions are summarized under general categories in the international account. Unlike the NIPAs, which are constructed according to a double-entry bookkeeping system where the two sides of an account theoretically equal the same value, in the International Transactions Account all entries are listed in a single account, with some entries of positive sign and some of negative. The total, then, should equal zero; however, due to imperfection in source data, statistical discrepancy must be accounted for as well.

To compile the balance of payments account, the BEA must merge and reconcile data collected internally with data from a number of other sources. Some data are provided by government agencies, including the Census Bureau, Customs, the Maritime Administration, the Immigration and Naturalization Service, and the Treasury department. Private records of U.S. multinational corporations are also examined and included in the compilation of the balance of payments.

International transactions track all exports and imports of goods, services, and income plus net U.S. assets abroad and net foreign assets in the United States. The balance of payments transactions are divided into current and capital accounts. Current account transactions incorporate imports and exports of goods and services adjusted for unilateral transfers. Unilateral transfers refer to payments, such as government grants, for which no services are currently rendered. The balance on current account is used widely to compare countries' relative strengths and weaknesses in international transactions. Capital account transactions cover savings and investment items, recording the purchase and sale of assets, including long- and short-term loans by private citizens and the government. International transactions are also divided into the broad categories of U.S. assets abroad and foreign assets in the United States. U.S. assets abroad include official reserves and other government and private assets. Foreign assets in the United States include the assets of official foreign agencies and other foreign assets.[6]

Table 6-6 provides an overview of U.S. international transactions. This summary table shows the U.S. international transactions as the value (in millions of U.S. dollars, seasonally adjusted) exports of goods and services less imports of goods and services and unilateral transfers, net U.S. assets abroad, and net foreign assets in the United States. The ten detailed accounts also outline U.S. international transactions, U.S. merchandise trade, service transactions, government transactions, direct investments, securities transactions, claims and liabilities to unaffiliated foreigners by U.S. nonbanking concerns, claims on foreigners reported by U.S. banks, foreign assets in the United States reported by U.S. banks, and U.S. international transactions by geographic area.

Table 6-6. Summary of U.S. International Transactions, 3rd Quarter 1990, in Millions of Dollars, Seasonally Adjusted

Exports of goods, services, and income	603,169
Merchandise, excluding military	360,465
Services	115,169
Income receipts on investments	127,536
Imports of goods, services, and income	−698,483
Merchandise, excluding military	−475,329
Services	−94,706
Income receipts on investments	−128,448
Unilateral transfers	−14,720
U.S. assets abroad, net (increase/capital outflow[−])	−127,061
U.S. official reserve assets, net	−25,293
U.S. government assets, other than official reserve assets, net	1,185
U.S. private assets	−102,953
Foreign assets in the United States, net (increase/capital inflow [+])	214,652
Foreign official assets, net	8,823
Other foreign assets, net	205,829
Allocation of special drawing rights	
Statistical discrepancy	22,443

Source: U.S. Bureau of Economic Analysis, *Survey of Current Business* (December 1990), p. 30.

Publication

Current quarterly and annual estimates are initially reported in the BEA *Reports* series. Official publication is in the March, June, September, and December issues of *Survey of Current Business*. Some data are provided as both seasonally adjusted and unadjusted. Figures for a given quarter are first released as preliminary data and later revised as more complete information is reported to the BEA for inclusion in its estimates. Revised estimates for the previous four years are published each June.

Caveats and Limitations

Given the complexity of foreign trade data, there are a number of caveats for potential data users. Of course, precise attention must be paid to the exact methodology and nomenclature employed by a given publication. For example, figures for the total U.S. trade deficit in 1984 range from $101.5 billion (for the current account deficit) to $123.3 billion (for the C.I.F. merchandise trade deficit), depending on the specific data series consulted.[7] The large range of difference between these two data series is accounted for by the comprehensiveness of the definition of "trade" and the valuation methodology employed (whether the cost of insurance and shipping is included). It is also important to remember that data reported under a given nomenclature are not directly comparable to data reported under other methodologies. However, concordances or conversion tables exist to facilitate comparison between schedules.[8]

It is important to note that revised U.S. foreign trade figures are released in several ways; however, the revisions are not as readily available as the initial figures released in the major FT series. U.S. export and import figures are adjusted on a monthly basis for carryover. Carryover refers to any trade documents received too late for inclusion in the figures for the month in which the transaction actually occurred. These revised figures appear only in *FT900: Highlights of U.S. Export and Import Trade*. Quarterly revisions are issued free upon request in the form of errata sheets, and an annual report summarizing all changes from the preceding calendar year is issued. Finally, revisions are sometimes issued in the form of a special announcement such as a press release.[9]

For analysis of the aggregate U.S. trade situation, both census and BEA figures are available. It is important to note how these two sets of data fundamentally differ from one another. The Census Bureau figures measure only merchandise trade; BEA data cover all foreign and international transactions, including merchandise, services, investments, government grants, and so on. Therefore, the BEA's measures provide broader coverage of the U.S. position in the international economy. In addition, even when calculating the U.S. balance of merchandise trade, both agencies provide differing data. Where the Census Bureau gives a figure of −$132,100,000,000 for the merchandise trade balance in 1985, the BEA's figure for the same period is −$122,148,000,000.[10] While the BEA's merchandise trade data are based on Census Bureau estimates, the BEA adjusts both valuation and coverage to conform to its accounting standards.

The general concept of foreign trade reflects only the movement of merchandise across national borders. Changes of ownership are not taken into account. According to some sources, as much as one-third of world trade is actually intracompany trade by multinational corporations. In 1985, exports by U.S. companies to foreign affiliates accounted for 32.6 percent of total exports, and imports from those affiliates into the United States accounted for 20.3 percent of total imports. It has been suggested that this sort of trade should not be considered foreign trade in the traditional sense. It is difficult to conceive how the U.S. trade position might change if intracompany transfers between both U.S. companies and their foreign affiliates and the transfers between foreign companies and their U.S. affiliates were excluded from the trade balance.[11]

In recent years, the accuracy of U.S. trade figures has been called into question. The Census Bureau admits that U.S. exports to Canada have been significantly and chronically underreported. The problem stems from the difficulty in tracking exports from the United States into Canada by shippers. Many shippers simply never file the required export documents. The problem was so severe that in 1986 the statistical discrepancy between U.S. figures on exports to Canada and the more accurate Canadian figures on imports from the United States was almost $11 billion. To correct this discrepancy, the U.S. export figures were revised to conform with Canadian data. This adjustment represented a 42 percent reduction in the total U.S. trade deficit. In 1988, the Census Bureau adopted a new procedure to correct for this problem. Now all U.S. export figures to Canada are based on the reporting by shippers to the U.S. Customs Bureau, but are adjusted to match the reporting of U.S. imports to Canada by Canadian government sources.[12]

A 1988 study by the Federal Reserve Bank of St. Louis suggests that there is reason to believe that total U.S. merchandise exports may be similarly underreported. This study builds the case that inaccuracies in reporting for the current accounts (which includes imports and exports of goods and services) have caused a large statistical discrepancy in the balance of payments since the 1970s. The study asserts that if all U.S. exports were corrected to reflect foreign national data on imports from the United States, U.S. official export figures would be substantially higher than those reported. This adjustment would, in turn, reduce the overall U.S. trade deficit.[13]

Likewise, there are inaccuracies in the capital accounts of the balance of payments. These inaccuracies are attributable largely to unreported capital transfers (e.g., foreign purchases of U.S. real estate or foreign deposits in U.S. financial institutions that escape reporting in the international transactions account). Capital movements, particularly in the private nonbank financial sector, tend to be imprecisely recorded and difficult to track. Some capital transfers go unreported in the account simply because changes in the ownership of real estate and capital investments are hard to track comprehensively. There are also added complications in cases of capital flight. Capital flight occurs most often in countries with political or financial crises or strict capital controls. In such cases, there is a great incentive to move money untraced to more stable (and less strictly controlled) locations. The high inflation experienced in Mexico in the late 1970s and early 1980s caused a capital flight problem for that country between 1980 and 1983. The media reports of the vast and large investments of the Marcos family in U.S. capital assets provide another high-profile example of this type of capital flight.[14]

Notes

1. U.S. Bureau of Economic Analysis, *Business Statistics: 1986* (Washington, D.C.: U.S. Government Printing Office, December 1987), p.78–85; and U.S. Congress, Joint Economic Committee, *1980 Supplement to Economic Indicators* (Washington, D.C.: U.S. Government Printing Office, 1980),

p.129–32; Victor R. Bailey and Sara R. Bowden, *Understanding United States Foreign Trade Data* (Washington, D.C.: U.S. Government Printing Office, August 1985), p.4–5; and U.S. Bureau of the Census, *FT135: U.S. General Imports for Consumption* (Washington, D.C.: Government Printing Office, 1988), p.1-1.

2. Bailey and Bowden, *Understanding United States Foreign Trade Data*, p.4–5.
3. Victor R. Bailey and Sara R. Bowden, "Understanding United States Foreign Trade Data," *Business America,* October 14, 1985, p.4.
4. Bailey and Bowden, *Understanding United States Foreign Trade Data*, p.6–7.
5. U.S. Bureau of Economic Analysis, *Business Statistics: 1986*, p.246–50.
6. _____ , *Survey of Current Business* (Washington, D.C.: U.S. Government Printing Office, September 1987), p.32–55; and Dominick Salvatore, "The Balance of Payments," in *Handbook of Economic and Financial Measures,* ed. Frank J. Fabozzi and Harry L. Greenfield (Homewood, Ill.: Dow Jones-Irwin, 1984), p.217–42.
7. Bailey and Bowden, "Understanding United States Foreign Trade Data," p.2.
8. Bailey and Bowden, *Understanding United States Foreign Trade Data*, p.33.
9. U.S. Bureau of the Census, *FT410: U.S. Exports—Schedule E Commodity by Country* (Washington, D.C.: U.S. Government Printing Office, May 1988), p.8.
10. U.S. Bureau of the Census, *Statistical Abstract of the United States* (Washington, D.C.: U.S. Government Printing Office, 1991), p.791, 804.
11. John Hein, "What the Trade Numbers Hide," *Across the Board*, February 23, 1987, p.12–13.
12. Mack Ott, "Is Trade Deficit as Big as It Seems?" *Wall Street Journal*, December 23, 1987, p.14.
13. Mack Ott, "Have U.S. Exports Been Larger Than Reported?" *Federal Reserve Bank of St. Louis Review*, September/October 1988, p.3.
14. John T. Cuddington, "Capital Flight: Estimates, Issues, Explanations," *Princeton University Studies in International Finance No. 58* (Princeton, N.J.: Princeton University Press, 1986) p.1–5.

Bibliography

Bailey, Victor R., and Sara R. Bowden. "Understanding United States Foreign Trade Data." *Business America* (October 14, 1985), p.2–7.
_____ . *Understanding United States Foreign Trade Data*. Washington, D.C.: U.S. Government Printing Office, August 1985.
Blades, Derek. "International Statistics: An OECD View." *Business Economics* (July 1986), p.37–42.
"Census Changes U.S. Trade Data Reporting." *Business America* (November 11, 1985), p.11.
Crudele, John. "Are Trade Statistics Fudged?" *San Francisco Examiner* (August 21, 1988).
Cuddington, John T. "Capital Flight: Estimates, Issues, Explanations." *Princeton University Studies in International Finance No. 58*. Princeton, N.J.: Princeton University Press, 1986.

"Does Anybody Really Know How the Economy Is Doing?" *Business Week* (May 6, 1985), p.128–29.

Hazelton, Walter A. "The Ins and Outs of Foreign Trade." *Management Accounting* (December 1987), p.53–58.

Hein, John. "What the Trade Numbers Hid." *Across the Board* (February 23, 1987), p.12–13.

Moczar, Louis J. *Status Report on Statistical and Methodological Improvements in the U.S. Balance of Payments Statistics*. BEA Working Paper No. 6. Atlanta, Ga.: Economic and Statistical Analysis/BEA, 1988.

O'Hara, Federick M., Jr. *Handbook of United States Economic and Financial Indicators*. Westport, Conn.: Greenwood Press, 1985, p.178–80.

Ott, Mack. "Have U.S. Exports Been Larger Than Reported?" *Federal Reserve Bank of St. Louis Review* (September/October 1988), p.3–23.

———. "Is Trade Deficit as Big as It Seems?" *Wall Street Journal* (December 23, 1987), p.14.

Salvatore, Dominick. "The Balance of Payments." In *Handbook of Economic and Financial Measures*, p.217–42. Homewood, Ill.: Dow Jones-Irwin, 1984.

U.S. Bureau of Economic Analysis. *BEA Reports: International Reports*. Washington, D.C.: U.S. Government Printing Office, fifteen times per year.

———. *Business Statistics*. Washington, D.C.: U.S. Government Printing Office, biennially.

———. *Foreign Transactions*. BEA Methodology Paper No. 3. Washington, D.C.: U.S. Government Printing Office, 1987.

———. *Survey of Current Business*. Washington, D.C.: U.S. Government Printing Office, monthly.

———. *A User's Guide to BEA Information*. Washington, D.C.: U.S. Government Printing Office, irregularly.

U.S. Bureau of the Census. *Census Catalog and Guide*. Washington, D.C.: U.S. Government Printing Office, 1988, p.91–105.

———. *Factfinder for the Nation: Foreign Trade Statistics. CFF No.14*. Washington, D.C.: U.S. Government Printing Office, March 1978.

———. *FT135: U.S. General Imports and Imports for Consumption—Schedule A Commodity by Country*. Washington, D.C.: U.S. Government Printing Office, monthly.

———. *FT150: U.S. General Imports—Commodity Groupings by World Region*. Washington, D.C.: U.S. Government Printing Office, annually.

———. *FT155: U.S. General Imports and Exports—World Area and Country of Origin by Schedule A Commodity Groupings*. Washington, D.C.: U.S. Government Printing Office, annually.

———. *FT246: U.S. Imports for Consumption and General Imports: TSUSA Commodity by Country of Origin*. Washington, D.C.: U.S. Government Printing Office, annually.

———. *FT410: U.S. Exports—Schedule E Commodity by Country*. Washington, D.C.: U.S. Government Printing Office, monthly.

———. *FT446: U.S. Exports—Schedule B Commodity by Country*. Washington, D.C.: U.S. Government Printing Office, annually.

———. *FT450: U.S. Exports—Schedule E Commodity Groupings by World Area*. Washington, D.C.: U.S. Government Printing Office, annually.

———. *FT455: U.S. Exports—World Area by Schedule E Commodity Grouping.* Washington, D.C.: U.S. Government Printing Office, annually.

———. *FT900: Summary of U.S. Export and Import Merchandise Trade.* Washington, D.C.: U.S. Government Printing Office, monthly.

———. *FT990: Highlights of U.S. Export and Import Trade.* Washington, D.C.: U.S. Government Printing Office, monthly.

———. *Guide to Foreign Trade Statistics.* Washington, D.C.: U.S. Government Printing Office, 1983.

———. *U.S. Foreign Trade Highlights.* Washington, D.C.: U.S. Government Printing Office, annually.

———. *U.S. Foreign Trade Statistics Classifications and Cross-Classifications.* Washington, D.C.: U.S. Government Printing Office, 1981.

U.S. Congress, Joint Economic Committee. *Maintaining the Quality of Economic Data.* 97th Congress, 1st session, Joint Committee Print. Washington, D.C.: U.S. Government Printing Office, 1981.

———. *The Quality of the Nation's Economic Statistics: Hearing, March 17–April 17, 1986.* Washington, D.C.: U.S. Government Printing Office, 1986.

———. *1980 Supplement to Economic Indicators: Historical and Descriptive Background.* Washington D.C.: U.S. Government Printing Office, p.129–32.

"Views Differ over Japan Trade Data." *Asian Wall Street Journal* (March 3, 1988).

Wolf, Charles, Jr. "Who Owes Whom and How Much?" *Wall Street Journal* (January 6, 1988), p.14.

7   Federal Government Finance

The federal budget is perhaps the single most important U.S. public document. Since 1922, the year of the first centralized, unified budget, this document has served as a key barometer of federal policy. The allocation of federal funds for specific programs and services, as authorized by the budget, is one tangible measure of federal policies and priorities. In recent years, the growing federal budget deficit has increasingly become a cause for debate and concern.

Several agencies including the Office of Management and Budget (OMB), the BEA, and the Bureau of the Census, produce data on federal government finance. The range of available data includes information on actual and proposed receipts and outlays, as well as budget estimates based on fixed economic projections. In addition, some data are calculated on a calendar-year basis, while others are calculated on a fiscal-year basis. Each type of data is produced under a different set of operating assumptions for different purposes. Informed use of federal government finance data requires an awareness of the range of data sources.

OMB Budget Data

The OMB is the lead executive agency in the federal budget process. The OMB controls the administration of the federal budget and provides the President with analyses and recommendations on budget proposals. This charge includes responsibility for the preparation of the President's budget and the development of a variety of background data to support the informed analysis and consideration of budget proposals.

History

Until fiscal year 1922, the federal government did not have a centralized budgeting office or a unified budget procedure. Instead, each agency prepared its own budget and transmitted it to the Treasury department for submission to Congress. Congress generally passed these agency budgets without substantive review. The Budget and Accounting Act of 1921 established the Bureau of the Budget and the first centrally prepared federal budget. With the fiscal year 1923 budget, the federal government moved to a centrally prepared budget covering all important activities of the executive branch, subject to Presidential scrutiny and Congressional review. Excluded from this comprehensive budget were the receipts and expenditures of the federal trust funds (e.g., the Unemployment Trust Funds and Social Security Trust Fund) and those of government corporations (e.g., the Pension Benefit Guarantee Corporation). Trust funds collect certain taxes or other receipts for use in carrying out specific purposes or programs in accordance with the terms of a trust agreement or statute. This new budget was known as the administrative budget, and it remained the primary budget document until after World War II. [1]

Another important change in federal budget procedure came with the 1936 budget. In that year, the functional classification of budget expenditures was introduced. For the first time, expenditures were grouped by broad functions, often cutting across agency or departmental lines. The exact categories and terminology used in the classification scheme have changed over the years; however, broad groupings have generally included such functions as national defense, international affairs and finance, natural resources, community development and housing, veterans benefits and services, and several others. [2] The most recent functional classifications are given here as Table 7-1.

The budget for fiscal year 1957 contained the first consolidated cash statement. The consolidated cash statement included federal receipts from and payments to the public. It was more comprehensive than the administrative budget, covering the activities of the administrative budget, as well as the operations of the trust accounts and the transactions of several government enterprises that were excluded from the administrative budget. This new budget document provided a much more comprehensive measure of federal finance and cash flows between the federal government and the remainder of the economy. [3]

Over time, numerous changes have been made in the budget coverage and in the accounting practices underlying the federal budget. Among the most significant changes in the past several decades was the adoption of a fully unified budget, first issued in January 1968. Under the unified budget concept, all federal monies—both federal funds and trust funds—are included in one comprehensive budget. Unlike

Table 7-1. Functional Classifications for the Federal Budget

Category	Subcategories	Category	Subcategories
National Defense	Department of Defense—Military	Medicare	Medicare
	Atomic Energy Defense Activities	Income Security	General Retirement and Disability
	Defense-related Activities		Insurance (excluding Social Security)
International Affairs	International Development and		Federal Employee Retirement and
	Humanitarian Assistance		Disability
	International Security Assistance		Unemployment Compensation
	Conduct of Foreign Affairs		Housing Assistance
	Foreign Information and Exchange		Food and Nutrition Assistance
	Activities		Other Income Assistance
	International Financial Programs	Social Security	Social Security
General Science,	General Science and Basic Research	Veterans Benefits and	Income Security for Veterans
Space, and	Space Flight	Services	Veterans Education, Training, and
Technology	Space Science, Applications, and		Rehabilitation
	Technology Supporting		Hospital and Medical Care for
	Space Activities		Veterans
Energy	Energy Supply		Veterans Housing
	Energy Conservation		Other Veterans Benefits and Services
	Emergency Energy Preparedness	Administration of Justice	Federal Law Enforcement Activities
	Energy Information, Policy, and		Federal Litigation and Judicial
	Regulation		Activities
Natural Resources	Water Resources		Federal Correctional Activities
and Environment	Conservation and Land Management		Criminal Justice Assistance
	Recreational Resources	General Government	Legislative Functions
	Pollution Control and Abatement		Central Fiscal Operations
	Other Natural Resources Programs		General Property and Records
Agriculture	Farm Income Stabilization		Management
	Agricultural Research and Services		Central Personnel Management
Commerce and	Mortgage Credit and Deposit		General Purpose Fiscal Assistance
Housing Credit	Insurance		Other General Government
	Postal Service		Deductions for Offsetting Receipts
	Other Advancement of Commerce	Net Interest	Interest on the Public Debt
Transportation	Ground Transportation		Interest Received by On-Budget Trust
	Air Transportation		Funds
	Water Transportation		Interest Received by Off-Budget Trust
	Other Transportation		Funds
Community and	Community Development		Other Interest
Regional Development	Area and Regional Development	Allowances	Employee Health Benefits Reform
Education, Training,	Elementary, Secondary, and		Reduced Government Mail Rates
Employment, and	Vocational Education		Allowances for Contingencies
Social Services	Higher Education	Undistributed	G-R-H Aggregate Spend-Out
	Research and General Education Aids	Offsetting Receipts	Requirement
	Training and Employment		Employer Share, Employee
	Other Labor Services		Retirement (On-Budget)
	Social Services		Employer Share, Employee
Health	Health Care Services		Retirement (Off-Budget)
	Health Research		Rents and Royalties in the Outer
	Education and Training of Health		Continental Shelf
	Care Work Force		Sales of Major Assets
	Consumer and Occupational Health		Other Undistributed Offsetting
	and Safety		Receipts

Source: U.S. Office of Management and Budget, *Budget of the United States Government: Fiscal Year 1991* (Washington, D.C.: U.S. Government Printing Office, 1990).

trust funds, federal funds are derived mainly from taxes and borrowing and are not restricted by law to any specific government purpose. While trust fund receipts and outlays were included in the unified budget, prior to the Balanced Budget and Emergency Deficit Control Act of 1985 (or Gramm-Rudman-Hollings, G-R-H, as it is popularly known), the receipts and outlays of the trusts were off-budget for the purpose of balancing the budget. Subsequent to the passage of G-R-H, all formerly off-budget entities are treated as on-budget for the purpose of deficit calculation, with the exception of Social Security which remains off-budget. [4]

The Budget Process

The Congressional Budget and Impoundment Act of 1974 created the Congressional Budget Office (CBO). This act also established a timetable and procedures for the Congressional budget process. Recent legislation, largely G-R-H and the Omnibus Budget Reconciliation Act, has modified the federal budget process. The revised budget process is as follows.

As the initial step in the budget process, the President submits his budget for the following fiscal year (beginning October 1) to Congress early in the calendar year. This budget provides information on the activities and functions of the government, estimated expenditures, and proposed appropriations. [5] Five days before this budget is submitted to Congress, the CBO issues a sequestration preview report containing up-to-date estimates of the maximum deficit amount and the discretionary spending limits on the basis of the CBO's (or Congress's) view of the economy. As the budget is issued, the OMB must issue its own sequestration preview report that provides the Presidential view of the likely deficit and spending limits based on its own (or the President's) view of the economy and deficit levels. The House and Senate budget committees prepare a concurrent resolution that is the tentative Congressional budget. This resolution is referred to appropriate Congressional committees in both houses for their review and recommendations. The resolution sets the target for total appropriations, outlays, and taxes, and breaks down the budget by the functional categories outlined in Table 7-1. The resolution does not set funding levels for individual agencies or programs. [6]

On the basis of the budget resolution, thirteen appropriations bills are drawn up. These bills outline actual allocations for individual agencies and programs. The appropriations process is handled by the appropriations committees of each house of Congress. Each committee has thirteen subcommittees that handle appropriations for different governmental departments. Congress is to adopt a budget resolution by April 15. The budget is then transmitted to the President for signature. On October 1, the fiscal year begins and the budget takes effect. [7]

Following the passage of G-R-H, an additional step was added to the budget process. This is the sequestration process. Under G-R-H, a timetable of set deficit targets was established. The timetable was designed to achieve forced deficit reduction and a balanced budget through automatic sequestration of federal funds if the preset targets were not met. G-R-H was later amended by the Omibus Budget Reconciliation Act, which replaced the fixed deficit reduction targets with limits on discretionary spending (those budget items not fixed by other legislation) and flexible deficit targets. Under the 1990 amendments to the budget process, the OMB and CBO also issue update reports on the deficit and sequestration in August. These reports revise the information provided in the preview reports. If needed, the Presidential spending reduction order is issued fifteen days after the Congressional session ends. This order withholds spending authority for budgeted allocations in order to meet the deficit reduction targets.[8]

OMB Definitions

The OMB is responsible for recording federal receipts and outlays as part of its administrative management of the budget. The OMB has its own accounting system and requirements for the treatment and definition of federal financial transactions, as outlined below.

OMB records budget receipts less refunds. Entries are recorded on a cash basis with collections recorded upon receipt of the cash, and refunds recorded when the refund checks are issued. Budget receipts generally represent the amount of money (net of refunds) collected by the government from the public through the exercise of governmental or sovereign power. These receipts include taxes and compulsory social insurance contributions, as well as receipts from other sources, such as fees, fines, and deposits of earnings by the Federal Reserve System. The receipts also include noncompulsory collections of money that are similar, or closely related, to compulsory payments (such as supplementary medical insurance premiums).

All budget outlays (or expenditures) except interest on the public debt are also recorded on a cash basis. Interest on the public debt is recorded on an accrual basis. That is, interest incurred but not yet paid is counted as a budget outlay and as an increase in federal debt. Budget outlays include all payments for programs included in the budget and also include all offsetting collections. Offsetting collections fall into two broad categories. One type of offsetting collection occurs when receipts arise as payments from one government account to another. In that case, they are reflected as offsets to outlays rather than as budget receipts. The other type of offsetting collection is receipts from market transactions (sale of goods or services, etc.) rather than from the exercise of sovereign power. These funds are recorded as an offsetting adjustment to budget outlays rather than as receipts.[9]

A budget surplus exists whenever receipts exceed outlays. Conversely, the budget deficit is the amount by which total budget outlays for a fiscal year exceed total revenues.[10] Gross federal debt (or total debt) is composed of all currently outstanding federal obligations issued by the Treasury department. Whereas the budget deficit is the debt level attributable to an individual budget year, the total debt is the cumulative sum of all currently outstanding debts. Gross federal debt also includes all borrowing by federal agencies other than the Treasury and is the broadest measure of the federal debt. Total public debt includes only borrowing by the Treasury.[11]

Publication

Budget of the United States Government is produced by the OMB and transmitted by the President to Congress according to the previously outlined budget calendar. It contains the budget message of the President and presents an overview of his budget proposals. It also includes notes and appendixes that outline the economic assumptions under which it was compiled. A variety of supplemental statistical information is also provided. The bulk of the budget document is devoted to the detailed budget estimates. The budget was formerly published in six volumes. However, beginning with fiscal year 1991, *Budget of the United States Government* is published in a single volume that incorporates the information published in those six volumes in a revised form. The annual budget is updated by the release of monthly budget receipts and expenditures data in *Monthly Statement of Receipts and Expenditures of the United States Government*, issued by the Department of the Treasury.

Table 7-2 shows the budget authorities and appropriations for economic and statistical analysis programs of the Department of Commerce in fiscal year 1991. The budget document breaks down these appropriations by such specific categories as economic analysis, policy support, and Japanese technical literature. It also includes data for prior fiscal years. A brief narrative describes each of these categories.

The BEA's Governmental Finance Data

The BEA also produces government finance data as part of the NIPAs. The NIPAs are the most widely used measure of aggregate economic activity in the United States. Described in greater detail in chapter 5, the NIPAs track total economic activity for all sectors of the economy (business, government, household, and the rest of the world).

Table 7-2. Budget of the United States Government, Fiscal Year 1991

Economic and Statistical Analysis Federal Funds
Program and Financing (in Thousands of Dollars)

		1989 actual	1990 est.	1991 est.
Identification Code 13-1500-0-1-376				
	Program by activities:			
	Direct program:			
00.01	Economic analysis	24,577	25,611	34,260
00.02	Policy support	5,269	5,297	5,688
00.03	Productivity, technology, and innovation	2,052	—	—
00.04	Japanese technical literature	376	—	—
00.91	Total direct program	32,274	30,908	39,948
01.01	Reimbursable program	2,001	1,894	2,100
10.00	Total obligations	34,275	32,802	42,048
	Financing:			
	Offsetting collections from:			
11.00	Federal funds	−1,554	−1,505	−1,705
14.00	Non-federal sources	−447	−395	−395
25.00	Unobligated balance lapsing	625	—	—
27.00	Reduction purs. to PL 99-177	—	6	—
39.00	Budget authority	32,899	30,908	39,948
	Budget authority:			
40.00	Appropriation	32,899	31,150	39,948
40.00	Reduction purs. to PL99-177	—	−242	—
43.00	Appropriations (adjusted)	32,899	30,908	39,948
	Relation of obligations to outlays:			
71.00	Obligations incurred, net	32,274	30,902	39,948
72.40	Obligated balance, start of year	3,479	4,339	3,399
74.40	Obligated balance, end of year	−4,339	−3,399	−4,394
77.00	Adjustments in expired accounts	−254	—	—
90.00	Outlays	31,159	31,842	38,953

Source: U.S. Office of Management and Budget, *Budget of the United States Government: Fiscal Year 1991* (Washington, D.C.: U.S. Government Printing Office, 1990), p. A538.

Government Receipts and Expenditures (NIPAs)

There are five accounts in the NIPA system; it is the third account that records government receipts and expenditures. This account, provided as Table 7-3, measures the receipts and expenditures of federal, state, and local governments in the United States. The income side of the account is the total of government expenditures and surplus. It includes government purchases of goods and services, government transfer payments, net interest paid by government, payments of government subsidies, and government surpluses or deficits adjusted for dividends received

Table 7-3. NIPA Account Three: Government Receipts and Expenditures Account

Government expenditures and surplus	Government receipts
Purchases	Personal tax and nontax payments

Transfer payments
  To persons
  To rest of the world
Net interest paid
	Corporate profits tax liability
	Indirect business tax and nontax liability
	Contributions for social insurance
	  Employer
	  Personal

Less: dividends received by government	
Subsidies less current surplus of government enterprises	
Less: wage accruals less disbursements	

Surplus or deficit (−), national income and product accounts
  Federal
  State and local	

Source: U.S. Bureau of Economic Analysis, *Survey of Current Business* (October 1991), p. 28.

by government and wage accruals less disbursements. The product side summarizes government receipts as the total of personal tax and nontax payments, corporate profits tax liability, indirect business tax and nontax liability, and contributions for social insurance.

Federal Receipts and Expenditures (NIPAs)

The NIPA table that summarizes federal receipts and expenditures is provided here as Table 7-4. In the NIPAs, federal receipts are the sum of personal tax and nontax receipts (nontax receipts include estate and gift taxes and other nontax revenues), corporate profits taxes (from Federal Reserve Banks and others), indirect business taxes and nontax accruals (such as accruals of excise taxes, customs duties, and nontaxes), and contributions for social insurance. Expenditures are the sum of federal purchases of goods and services (for national defense and nondefense), transfer payments (to persons and the rest of the world), grants-in-aid to state and local governments, net interest paid (to persons, business, and the rest of the world less interest received by government), and subsidies less current surplus of government enterprises, adjusted for wage accruals less disbursements. Additional NIPA tables provide data for state and local government receipts and expenditures, government purchases of goods and services, and national defense expenditures.

NIPA estimates are recorded according to an accounting system designed to facilitate national income accounting and adhering to international standards that facilitate international comparability. NIPA data

Table 7-4. NIPA Federal Government Receipts and Expenditures, 1989

Receipts	*1,052.9*
Personal tax and nontax receipts	464.0
Income taxes	453.1
Estate and gift taxes	9.0
Nontaxes	1.8
Corporate profits tax accruals	110.4
Federal Reserve Banks	21.6
Other	88.8
Indirect business tax and nontax accruals	58.4
Excise taxes	34.1
Customs duties	17.5
Nontaxes	6.8
Contributions for social insurance	420.1
Expenditures	*1,187.2*
Purchases of goods and services	400.0
National defense	301.1
Nondefense	98.9
Transfer payments	471.9
To persons	458.6
To foreigners	13.4
Grants-in-aid to state and local governments	118.2
Net interest paid	172.0
Interest paid	191.7
To persons and business	155.7
To foreigners	36.0
Less: Interest received by government	19.6
Subsidies less current surplus of government enterprises	25.0
Subsidies	27.9
Less: current surplus of government enterprises	2.8
Less: wage accruals less disbursements	0
Surplus or deficit (−), national income and product accounts	−134.3
Social insurance funds	63.8
Other	−198.1

Source: U.S. Bureau of Economic Analysis, *Survey of Current Business* (December 1990), p. 8.

differ in several important ways from the OMB's federal budget accounting system delineated above. The statistical coverage of the NIPAs differs from the OMB's data in that these accounts include off-budget federal entities and exclude U.S. territories, lending transactions, and sales of physical and loan assets. The NIPAs are expressed on a calendar-year basis, whereas the OMB's budget is presented on a fiscal-year basis.

(The impact of this difference is discussed more fully in chapter 8.) There are also differences in the timing for recording transactions in the two systems. The NIPAs generally record personal taxes and Social Security insurance contributions when they are paid. Business taxes are recorded when they are accrued. In contrast, as previously noted, the budget records all receipts when they are received. In addition, the NIPAs record expenditures and outlays on a delivery basis, and the budget records them when cash is disbursed. Finally, netting differences arise because the budget records certain transactions as offsets to outlays, while the NIPAs record them as receipts, or vice versa. One such example is the treatment of government contributions to employee retirement.[12]

Publication

As noted in chapter 5, the quarterly and annual accounts of the NIPAs are published in *Survey of Current Business*. Quinquennial revisions are published in *National Income and Product Accounts of the United States: Statistical Tables*. In addition, select NIPA tables are provided in the budget document as appendixes to facilitate aggregate economic analysis.

Census Bureau's Federal Receipts and Expenditures

The Census Bureau conducts a quinquennial Census of Governments that provides comprehensive enumerative information on governmental finance for all levels of government. In addition, the Census Bureau conducts an annual survey of government finance that updates the census data.

As with the BEA's data, the Census Bureau's accounting system differs from that employed by the OMB. Financial transactions of government enterprises are included in federal budget figures only to the extent of their net effect (plus or minus) on the budget expenditures. However, census figures include gross revenue of government enterprises (other than loan investment transactions). Receipts treated in the federal budget as offsets against expenditures are counted as revenue and added back to the expenditure by the Census Bureau. The Census Bureau excludes the revenue and expenditure of trust funds handled on an agency basis for state and local governments (e.g., the state accounts in the unemployment fund, and the District of Columbia funds). Although interfund and intragovernmental transactions are netted out of federal budget totals, such transfer amounts are included in federal figures for various receipt and expenditure categories. Census figures exclude all such transfers. Whereas the federal budget treats interest expenditures on an accrual basis, the census records them on a disbursement basis. Finally, the

Census Bureau excludes the net excess of loan disbursements or loan repayments from expenditures and receipts.[13]

The functional classification used by the Bureau of the Census is also different from the classification used in *Budget of the United States Government*. Individual receipt items and expenditure amounts for various agencies and appropriation items are grouped according to two functional frameworks: one that categorizes revenues by source and one that categorizes expenditures by character. These frameworks are also used for reporting state and local government finances, thereby facilitating such comparisons better than the budget itself.

Federal Government Finances

Tables 7-5 and 7-6 provide summaries of federal government finance data from the Census Bureau. Table 7-5 includes data on revenue by source for fiscal year 1985-1986. Table 7-6 provides data on revenue and debt for the same period. The revenue and debt data are broken down by the Census Bureau's functional framework describing the character and object of the expenditure or debt. This classification scheme differs markedly from the programmatic breakdown provided in the budget as shown in Table 7-1.

Census GF Publication Series

The comprehensive *Census of Governments* is published approximately every five years. The Census Bureau's annual survey data are published in *Government Finances, Series GF*. The survey results are reported in eight volumes. Subject breakdowns for the series are given in Table 7-7. Report no. 5, *Government Finances,* summarizes the annual survey results. It is divided into nine sections: national summaries, state summaries, state revenues, state expenditures, debt and cash and securities holdings, utilities, finance by level of government for each state, finance and population and income, and population and personal income. The report provides financial data on a fiscal-year basis.

Budget Benchmarks

Throughout the budget process, policymakers and analysts attempt to gauge the impact of a given budget proposal on the economy (and vice versa). In addition to citing the proposed budget estimates, the official budget document, *Budget of the United States Government*, has historically presented alternate measures or baselines for use in comparing budget alternatives. These benchmarks are produced by the OMB and are theoretical budgets based on fixed economic projections. These projections

Table 7-5. Summary of Federal Government Finances 1985–1986: Revenue

Revenue	
Revenue, total	847,516
General revenue	580,611
General revenue from own sources	578,473
Taxes	471,898
Income	412,102
Individual	348,959
Corporation	63,143
Sales, gross receipts and customs	47,046
Customs duties	13,420
Motor fuel	11,641
Alcoholic beverages	5,601
Public utilities	5,047
Air transportation	2,708
Telephone	2,339
Tobacco products	4,608
Other sales and gross receipts taxes	6,729
Oil windfall profit tax	3,442
Motor vehicles, chassis and body	1,019
Tires, inner tubes, and tread rubber	286
Other categories not shown	1,910
Other taxes	12,750
Death and gift	6,958
All other	5,792
Charges and miscellaneous general revenue	106,575
Current charges	63,291
Postal receipts	29,099
National defense and international relations	6,774
Natural resources	14,705
Commodity Credit Corporation	2,815
Tennessee Valley Authority	4,304
Department of Interior, energy sales	2,252
Mineral ore and product sales	578
Timber sales	468
All other resource charges	4,288
Other current charges	12,713
Sale or property	2,697
Interest earnings	13,931
Other miscellaneous general revenue	26,656
Federal Reserve System, earnings	18,374
Continental shelf lands, lease and royalty	
revenue	4,716
Other	3,566
Insurance trust revenue	266,905
Social Security (OASDHI)	257,263
Employee retirement	4,541
Railroad retirement	4,184
Veterans' life insurance	686
Unemployment compensation	221

Source: U.S. Bureau of the Census, *Government Finances in 1985–86: Series GF-86, No. 5* (Washington, D.C.: U.S. Government Printing Office), p. 4–5.

Table 7-6. Summary of Federal Government Finances 1985–1986: Expenditure and Debt

Expenditure		Social services and income	
Expenditure, total	1,096,401	maintenance	
		Public welfare	25,790
By character and object		Hospitals	7,573
Intergovernmental expenditure	115,632	Public hospitals Veterans	6,185
Current operations	386,388	Other public hospitals	847
Capital outlay	85,647	Other hospitals	541
Construction	11,866	Health	7,520
Equipment	69,512	Social insurance administration	3,871
Land and existing structures	4,269	Veterans' services	17,139
Assistance and subsidies	64,375	Transportation	
Interest on debt	144,167	Highways	568
Insurance benefits	300,192	Air transportation	3,599
Exhibit: expenditure for salaries	123,054	Water transport and terminals	1,690
and wages		Public safety	
		Police protection	3,543
By function		Corrections	798
General expenditures	796,209	Environment and housing	
Intergovernment expenditure	115,632	Natural resources, parks	
Education	18,023	and recreation	60,075
Elementary and secondary education	3,268	Soil, water, mineral, and electric	
School breakfast and lunch	3,086	energy resources	15,358
Federal affected area assistance	674	Energy programs	5,995
Public welfare	44,544	Tennessee Valley Authority	3,951
Medical assistance	26,098	Army Corps of Engineers	1,891
Maintenance assistance	9,540	Soil Conservation Service	642
Child nutrition	439	Stabilization of farm prices	
Low-income energy assistance	2,842	and income	28,214
Health and hospitals	4,615	Commodity Credit Corporation	26,560
Special supplemental food		Farm credit programs	9,591
programs—WIC	1,710	Forestry	1,864
National Institutes of Health	666	Other agricultural resources	1,545
Highways	14,370	Other natural resources	2,049
Natural resources, parks and		National Oceanographic and	
recreation	2,424	Atmospheric Administration	1,246
Housing and community		Housing and community	
development	11,237	development	7,925
Other	20,419	Government administration	
Urban mass transportation	3,349	Financial administration	5,400
Contribution to District of Columbia	530	Judicial and legal	2,090
Direct expenditure	680,577	Other governmental administration	1,129
Selected federal programs		Interest on general debt	144,167
National defense and		General expenditure, n.e.c.	23,360
international relations	312,183	Insurance trust expenditure	300,192
Military functions	288,454	Social Security (OASDHI)	267,923
Economic assistance	7,788	Employee retirement	24,226
Atomic energy	7,602	Railroad retirement	5,969
Foreign affairs, n.e.c.	3,383	Veterans' life insurance	1,893
Food for freedom	1,095	Unemployment compensation	181
Military assistance	3,820		
Postal service	30,985	*Debt*	
Space research and technology	7,275	Gross debt outstanding at the end of	
Education services		the fiscal year	2,129,506
Education	13,581	Public debt	2,125,304
Veterans' education benefits	766	Federal agency debt	4,202
Other	12,815	Held by federal government	383,919
Libraries	316	Other debt outstanding	1,745,587

Source: U.S. Bureau of the Census, *Government Finances in 1985–86: Series GF-86, No. 5* (Washington, D.C.: U.S. Government Printing Office, 1987), p. 4-5.

Table 7-7. U.S. Bureau of the Census. Government Finances: Series GF

Series	Title
No. 1	*State Government Tax Collections*
No. 2	*Finances of Employee Retirement Systems of State and Local Governments*
No. 3	*State Government Finances*
No. 4	*City Government Finances*
No. 5	*Government Finances*
No. 6	*Local Government Finances in Major County Areas*
No. 7	*County Government Finances*
No. 8	*Finances of Public School Systems*

include such scenarios as the revenues and expenditures required to maintain current government services only, with no changes or additions to government programs, and the budget that might be supported in an economy operating at full employment. There is no intention that either of these baselines might be the actual budget put in place, but both provide good comparisons against which to measure a given budget proposal. In general, the nature of the baseline estimates to be submitted as part of the President's budget is mandated by law. The budget benchmarks are generated both during the budget process as well as after the budget is in place.

Prior to the passage of G-R-H, a number of budget benchmarks were produced. These included the current services budget (or budget baseline), which estimated federal taxes and spending on the assumption that current programs are continued without changes to policy, and the high employment budget, which assumed levels of economic activity that result in periods of high employment. With the adoption of G-R-H, only one alternate set of baseline estimates is prepared, the Gramm-Rudman-Hollings baseline budget. The G-R-H baseline budget reflects the future budget implications of current laws and regulations. The impact of new legislative initiatives is omitted. The budget levels of discretionary programs are based on prior appropriations adjusted for inflation and pay costs. The baseline also projects the level of the budget deficit.[14]

Data Limitations

Budget Baselines

While baseline budgets are useful in assessing proposed budgets, they are intended solely as benchmarks against which to measure such proposals. They are not intended as actual projections of federal receipts and expenditures or of economic activity under the baseline proposal. The relationship between federal receipts and expenditures, and economic performance is an interdependent one. That is, federal spending and taxation levels have a significant impact on economic performance, and economic performance influences actual federal revenues and spending. Were the baseline budget actually to be adopted, it would, in turn, influence economic activity and it is highly likely that this influence would affect the economy to such an extent that the baseline would not result in the levels of revenue, expenditure, or economic activity that are its theoretical basis.

In fact, the benchmark budget developed as part of G-R-H, contains scenarios that were never intended to become fiscal reality. For example, the cost of some one-time expenditures, such as the replacement of the space shuttle *Challenger*, was built into ongoing appropriations. In other instances, infrequent but recurring allocations, such as those for the decennial census, were totally unaccounted for in the baseline estimates. These baseline estimates were then used to calculate budget "cuts." For example, in fiscal year 1988, actual defense spending rose from $282 billion to $285.4 billion; however, this appropriation was considered to be a $5 billion cut from the calculated baseline budget. Under this system, federal spending rises every year, while the perception is that the budget has been cut. [15]

Trust Funds

As noted above, tax collections targeted to a specific purpose, such as Social Security, are held in federal government trust funds rather than in the federal general fund. Presently, trust fund expenditures (e.g., payment to Social Security beneficiaries) are treated as outlays for the purpose of the federal budget. Likewise, payments to and interest on trust funds are counted as budget receipts. Some experts argue that trust funds should be excluded from the budget and deficit calculations or be calculated separately from the administrative budget. This would radically alter the level of the budget deficit. For example, in 1990, the projected trust fund surplus amounted to approximately $134 billion. This surplus was used by the OMB to offset a deficit of about $250 billion. The counter argument maintains that treating the trust funds as separate from the federal budget would distort the overall picture of government finance that the budget and the deficit calculation attempts to provide. [16]

Government-Sponsored Enterprises

Similar to its use of trust funds, Congress sometimes chooses to carry out mandated programs through government-sponsored enterprises (GSEs), which operate outside the traditional government infrastructure. Some examples of GSEs include the National Railroad Passenger Corporation (Amtrak), the Pennsylvania Avenue Development Corporation, the Pension Benefit Guarantee Corporation, and the Tennessee Valley Authority. Some of these GSEs are self-supporting (like the Pension Benefit Guarantee Corporation); others (like Amtrak) obtain government assistance. The practice of establishing GSEs has recently come under criticism as political maneuvering intended to move controversial programs outside the control of the budget process, thereby moving large expenditures outside the formula for calculating the federal budget deficit. The prime example in this regard is the Resolution Trust Corporation, which was created in 1989 to handle the government's saving and loan bailout. The corporation was established to manage and resolve failed savings associations that were insured by the Federal Savings and Loan Insurance Act. The corporation fulfills the government's obligation to federally insured depositors and disposes of the assets of these institutions. While the bailout is partially financed through the sale of assets, a considerable portion of the cost is funded by Congressional appropriation, and these costs are moved outside the calculation of the budget deficit when funneled through a GSE.[17]

Capital Expenditures vs. Operating Budget

Another area of debate over the federal budget is the treatment of outlays. Under current procedures, government expenditures are classified as outlays without regard to the purpose of the expenditures, or the items being purchased. This means that the purchase of expendable goods, such as office supplies, is considered as equal to expenditures for items that have asset value, such as real estate, automobiles, research and development, or infrastructure. In private industry, these expenditures would instead be viewed as two distinct types of outlay: the former as current expenses, the latter as long-term investment. If federal and private finances were calculated by the same standard, the federal government's financial picture would be perceived very differently than is currently the case.[18]

Notes

1. Michael E. Levy, "Federal Budget," in *Encyclopedia of Economics*, ed. Douglas Greenwald (New York: McGraw-Hill, 1982), p.369.
2. Ibid., p.370–72.
3. Ibid., p.369–70.
4. U.S. Bureau of the Census, *Statistical Abstract of the United States* (Washington, D.C.: U.S. Government Printing Office, 1990), p.307.

5. U.S. House, Committee on the Budget, *The Congressional Budget Process: A General Explanation* (Washington, D.C.: U.S. Government Printing Office, 1986), p.11.

6. Levy, "The Federal Budget," p.375; and U.S. Congress, Congressional Budget Office, *The Economic and Budget Outlook: Fiscal Years 1992–1996* (Washington, D.C.: U.S. Government Printing Office, 1991), p.52–53.

7. U.S. House, Committee on the Budget, *The Congressional Budget Process*, p.15.

8. U.S. Congress, Congressional Budget Office, *The Economic and Budget Outlook*, p.54.

9. U.S. Congress, Joint Economic Committee, *Supplement to Economic Indicators* (Washington, D.C.: U.S. Government Printing Office, 1980), p.115–16.

10. U.S. Office of Management and Budget, *Budget of the United States Government* (Washington, D.C.: U.S. Government Printing Office, 1991), p.A1231–A1232.

11. U.S. Bureau of the Census, *Statistical Abstract*, p.307.

12. U.S. Office of Management and Budget, *Budget of the United States Government*, p.A81.

13. U.S. Bureau of the Census, *Government Finances in 1985–86* (Washington, D.C.: U.S. Government Printing Office, 1987), p.xv.

14. U.S. Office of Management and Budget, *Budget of the United States Government*, p.A27–A28.

15. Lawrence J. Haas, "Budget Focus," *National Journal,* January 2, 1988, p.49.

16. U.S. General Accounting Office, *The Budget Treatment of Trust Funds*, GAO/T-AFMD-90-3 (Washington, D.C.: U.S. Government Printing Office, 1989), p.2–3.

17. Ibid.

18. Henry Kelly and Andrew Wyckoff, "Distorted Image: How Government Statistics Misrepresent the Economy," *Technology Review*, February/March 1989, p.55–57.

Bibliography

Collender, Stanley. *The Guide to the Federal Budget Fiscal 1991*. Washington, D.C.: Urban Institute Press, 1990.

Eisner, Robert, and Paul J. Pieper. "How to Make Sense of the Deficit." In *A Nation in Debt*, p.87–101. Frederick, Md.: University Publications of America, 1987.

Haas, Lawrence J. "Budget Focus." *National Journal* (January 2, 1988), p.49.

Hansen, Eric. "Introduction to the U.S. Congressional Budget Process." *Government Publications Review* (May/June 1989), p.219–38.

Herman, Edward. *The Federal Budget: A Guide to Process and Principal Publications*, (Ann Arbor, Mich.: Pierian Press, 1991).

Kelly, Henry, and Andrew Wyckoff, "Distorted Image: How Government Statistics Misrepresent the Economy." *Technology Review* (February/March 1989), p.53–60.

Levy, Michael E. "Federal Budget." In *Encyclopedia of Economics*, p.369–72. Ed. Douglas Greenwald. New York: McGraw-Hill, 1982.

Passel, Peter. "Economic Scene: Deficits Quack, Politicians Duck." *New York Times* (May 30, 1990).

Schrer, Joseph. "Government Deficits and the Budget." In *Handbook of Economic and Financial Measures*, p.199–216. Homewood, Ill.: Dow Jones-Irwin, 1984.

U.S. Bureau of the Census. *Government Finances Series (Series GF)*. Washington, D.C.: U.S. Government Printing Office, annually.

———. *Statistical Abstract of the United States*. Washington, D.C.: U.S. Government Printing Office, annually.

U.S. Congress. House. Committee on the Budget. *The Congressional Budget Process: A General Explanation*. Washington, D.C.: U.S. Government Printing Office, 1986.

U.S. Congress. Joint Economic Committee. *Supplement to Economic Indicators*. Washington, D.C.: U.S. Government Printing Office, 1980, p.115–24.

U.S. Congress. Senate. Committee on the Budget. *Congressional Budget Act Annotated*. 101st Congress, 2d session, Senate Print 101–86. Washington, D.C.: U.S. Government Printing Office, February 1990.

U.S. General Accounting Office. *The Budget Treatment of Trust Funds*. GAO/T-AFMD-90-3. Washington, D.C.: U.S. Government Printing Office, 1989.

———. *A Glossary of Terms Used in the Federal Budget Process*. 3rd ed. Washington, D.C.: U.S. Government Printing Office, March 1981.

U.S. Office of Management and Budget. *Budget of the United States Government*. Washington, D.C.: U.S. Government Printing Office, annually.

Data Compilation and Presentation

There are various procedures and techniques that are employed in the compilation and presentation of statistical data. Procedures used in this compilation process that affect the use of the data include such basic ones as questionnaire design and sampling procedures. These procedures and techniques may apply to a broad range of statistical data, including the specific measures examined in the first seven chapters of this book. Presentation techniques of importance to data users include revision of estimates, seasonal adjustment, and indexing. Data producers must make decisions regarding how data will be compiled and presented. Once those decisions have been made and implemented, they have an impact on the selection and applicability of the data in secondary analysis by other data users. Methods of data compilation, presentation, and publication have the potential to affect research and reference strategies. This chapter will examine a number of factors that bear upon the usefulness and relative accuracy of statistical data and will provide illustrative examples from well-known and often-used statistical sources.

Currency of Data Sources

At the simplest level, the selection of the publication to be consulted will have a significant impact on the currency of data provided. In instances where timeliness is important, this will affect the usefulness of statistical data. Figures for widely tracked statistical series appear in a number of well-known sources. Official sources generally include printed and online (computerized or telephone) press releases, official periodical sources such as *Federal Reserve Bulletin* and *Survey of Current Business*,

Table 8-1. Current Civilian Unemployment Rate as Given in Several Major Sources, as of Mid-July 1990

Source (issue date)	Rate (%)	Period covered
Wall Street Journal (July 9, 1990)	5.2	June 1990
Employment and Earnings (May 1990)	5.3	April 1990
Monthly Labor Review (April 1990)	5.3	1989 (annual)
Handbook of Labor Statistics (1989 annual)	5.5	1988 (annual)
Statistical Abstract (1990 annual)	5.5	1988 (annual)

and data compilations ranging from *Handbook of Labor Statistics* and *Economic Report of the President* to the *Statistical Abstract of the United States*. In addition, various privately published sources track important statistical series. Sources that provide recurring access to statistical data include most daily newspapers, as well as major business magazines such as *Business Week, Forbes*, and *Fortune*. Each of these sources can provide data for a number of important statistical series. However, given differences in the publication process and schedule for each source, there can be a significant difference in the currency of data provided for a given measure at a given point in time.

For example, several sources were consulted in mid-July 1990 in order to obtain the most current data on the unemployment rate. These included the official periodicals of the BLS, *Statistical Abstract*, as well as the BLS's own data compilation, *Handbook of Labor Statistics*. In addition, *The Wall Street Journal* was consulted for the dates immediately following the most recent scheduled release date for unemployment figures. The data obtained from these sources are outlined in Table 8-1. As the table demonstrates, the lag in currency ranged from ten days for press coverage of the prior month's unemployment figures in *The Wall Street Journal* to approximately eighteen months for the annual data provided in *Statistical Abstract* and *Handbook of Labor Statistics*.

Estimated Data and Revision of Estimates

Some important data series attempt to estimate very large-scale economic or demographic processes. For example, the Bureau of the Census provides a variety of information on the characteristics of the population of the United States. It is not practical to obtain this information by direct observation or enumeration more frequently than the Constitutionally mandated decennial census. Therefore, intercensal population data are generally estimates derived from examining, merging, and adjusting data from a number of sources that reflect the change in population, as well as from the sample CPS. Such sources might include prior census data, vital statistics records, and other sources such as employment records that provide information about population migration. Because these methods provide estimates rather than a complete enumeration, they are generally considered less reliable than an enumeration.

Estimated data series may be revised. This technique is employed when the timely release of the data series is critical to government and private analysts for use in decisions regarding government policy and private sector planning, and yet more accurate or additional source data frequently become available after initial estimates have been made. These new and improved data have the potential to provide improved estimates. In such instances, data producers may choose to balance the need for timely release against the need for the most accurate estimates possible by providing early rough estimates and then revising data series on a scheduled basis to provide more accurate estimates than were possible when initial figures were calculated and released. In such cases, later estimates are always considered more accurate, as they are based on improved source data.

Estimated Population Data

As stated above, intercensal population estimates are calculated based on a combination of existing data. These estimates are the result of comparing earlier census data with vital statistics and indicators of population migration. For example, Medicare statistics are sometimes used as a measure of change in the population older than age sixty-five. Population estimates are inherently subject to estimation error due to the fact that the correlation between source data used in the estimation process and population change itself is not perfect; therefore, estimated data must be considered less accurate than actual enumeration. This means that some judgments must be made as to the quality of estimates when used in comparison with data from the census. Estimates are consistent with the enumerative data that serve as their basis, but care must be used when comparing estimated data to other figures. Table 8-2 illustrates this point. In this table, population figures from the 1970 and 1980 censuses are compared with the population estimates based on the 1970 census for five states having a greater than 30 percent gain in population during the 1970s. The figures from the 1980 census appear to follow a pattern established in the estimates for Wyoming, Arizona, and Alaska. In the cases of Florida and Nevada, however, there are significant differences between the population estimates for July 1, 1979, and the enumerative data for April 1, 1980. While the population estimates were the only figures available prior to the 1980 census, the 1980 enumerative figures supersede the earlier estimates. In fact, for Florida and Nevada, the earlier estimates clearly reflect a different trend than

Table 8-2. Annual Estimates of the Resident Population of Selected States, 1970–1980 (in thousands)

Date	FL	WY	AZ	NV	AK
1970*	6,791	322	1,775	489	303
1970	6,851	334	1,795	494	305
1971	7,101	339	1,878	514	316
1972	7,407	345	1,975	535	326
1973	7,757	351	2,075	551	332
1974	8,087	362	2,156	573	343
1975	8,253	377	2,200	590	379
1976	8,348	392	2,244	610	405
1977	8,481	407	2,309	634	408
1978	8,861	425	2,373	666	411
1979	8,860	450	2,450	702	406
1980*	9,746	470	2,718	800	402

Sources: U.S. Bureau of the Census, *Population Estimates and Projections: Annual Estimates of the Population of States: July 1, 1970 to 1979: Current Population Reports: Series P-25, No. 876* (Washington, D.C.: U.S. Government Printing Office, February 1980). U.S. Bureau of the Census, *Characteristics of the Population: 1980 Census of Population: Series PC 80-1* (Washington, D.C.: U.S. Government Printing Office, 1984).
Note: Estimated data are for July 1 of the year indicated. Census data are for April 1 of the year indicated.
* Figures taken from *Characteristics of the Population,* noted above

the 1980 enumeration revealed, and should not be compared with the 1980 census figures.

Revision of Population Estimates

It is also important to note that estimates of the population are subject to revision. The Bureau of the Census, the agency responsible for official population figures, releases intercensal population estimates on a periodic basis, and later estimates are based on the most up-to-date information on population change. Therefore, it is important to use the most current estimates available. Table 8-3 illustrates this point. Data on the resident population of Alaska for the 1970s are provided. The estimates released throughout the decade are given and demonstrate the range of data available, depending on the source consulted. For example, the resident population of Alaska in 1975 was initially estimated in November of 1976 to be 352,000. However, by February of 1980, this estimate had been revised upward to 379,000—a revision of nearly 8 percent. In addition, the estimates fluctuated from a low of 352,000 to a high of 383,000 before the 379,000 estimate was reached.

Revision of GNP Estimates

The U.S. GNP is another estimated data series. Estimates for the GNP are revised on a regular basis. Before the 1992 benchmark revision, initial

Table 8-3. Annual Estimates of the Resident Population of Alaska, 1970–1979 (in thousands)

	As of 7/74	As of 1/75	As of 11/76	As of 12/76	As of 7/78	As of 12/78	As of 4/79	As of 11/79	As of 2/80
1970	304	–	304	–	305	–	–	–	305
1971	315	–	315	–	317	–	–	–	316
1972	325	–	325	–	326	–	–	–	326
1973	330(p)	330	331	–	333	–	–	–	332
1974	–	337	341	–	344	–	–	–	343
1975	–	–	352(p)	365	383	–	–	–	379
1976	–	–	–	382(p)	408	–	–	–	405
1977	–	–	–	–	407(p)	413	413	–	408
1978	–	–	–	–	–	403(p)	403(p)	411	411
1979	–	–	–	–	–	–	–	406(p)	406(p)

Sources: Estimates for 07/74 are taken from U.S. Bureau of the Census, "Estimates of the Population of States with Components of Change 1970 to 1973," *Current Population Reports: Series P-25, No. 520* (Washington, D.C.: U.S. Government Printing Office, 1974). Estimates for 01/75 are taken from U.S. Bureau of the Census, "Estimates of the Population of States by Age: July 1, 1973 and 1974," *Current Population Reports: Series P-25, No. 539* (Washington, D.C.: U.S. Government Printing Office, 1975). Estimates for 11/76 are taken from U.S. Bureau of the Census, "Estimates of the Population of States with Components of Change 1970 to 1975," *Current Population Reports: Series P-25, No. 640* (Washington, D.C.: U.S. Government Printing Office, 1976). Estimates for 12/76 are taken from U.S. Bureau of the Census, "Revised 1975 and Provisional 1976 Estimates of the Population of States, Components of Change, 1970 to 1976," *Current Population Reports: Series P-25, No. 642* (Washington, D.C.: U.S. Government Printing Office, 1976). Estimates for 07/78 are taken from U.S. Bureau of the Census, "Annual Estimates of the Population of States, July 1, 1970 to 1977 with Components of Change 1970 to 1977," *Current Population Reports: Series P-25, No. 727* (Washington, D.C.: U.S. Government Printing Office, 1978). Estimates for 12/78 are taken from U.S. Bureau of the Census, "Estimates of the Population of States: July 1, 1977 and 1978 (Advance Report)," *Current Population Reports: Series P-25, No. 790* (Washington, D.C.: U.S. Government Printing Office, 1978). Estimates for 04/79 are taken from U.S. Bureau of the Census, "Revised 1977 and Provisional 1978 Estimates of the Population of States and Components of Change," *Current Population Reports: Series P-25, No. 799* (Washington, D.C.: U.S. Government Printing Office, 1979). Estimates for 11/79 are taken from U.S. Bureau of the Census, "Estimates of the Population of States: July 1, 1978 and 1979 (Advance Report)," *Current Population Reports: Series P-25, No. 868* (Washington, D.C.: U.S. Government Printing Office, 1979). Estimates for 02/80 are taken from U.S. Bureau of the Census, "Annual Estimates of the Population of States: July 1, 1970 to 1979 with Components of Change, 1970 to 1979," *Current Population Reports: Series P-25, No. 876* (Washington, D.C.: U.S. Government Printing Office, 1980).
Note: Estimated data are for July 1 of the year indicated.
(p) indicates provisional estimates
– indicates estimate not made

preliminary estimates for a given month were released in the following month. These preliminary figures were generally revised in the following two months, as more and better source data become available. Revisions of the GNP for the three most recent years were announced in the July issue of the *Survey of Current Business*. Thereafter, revised figures were released in the quinquennial compilation *The National Income and Product Accounts of the United States: Statistical Tables*. Using the first quarter of 1982 as an example, Table 8-4 shows the initial preliminary estimates and subsequent revisions of the current dollar GNP. The initial estimate of $2,995.1 billion, made in April of 1982, has been revised by $117.5 billion as of the estimate released in 1986 in *The National Income and Product Accounts of the United States*. This represents a revision of approximately 4 percent.

Table 8-4. GNP Estimates for 1st Quarter 1982, Seasonally Adjusted at Annual Rates (in billions of dollars)

Source (issue date)	Current $ GNP
Survey of Current Business (April 1982)	2,995.1
Survey of Current Business (June 1982)	2,998.4
Survey of Current Business (July 1982)	2,995.5
Survey of Current Business (July 1983)	3,021.4
Survey of Current Business (July 1984)	3,026.0
The NIPAs of the US, 1929-82	3,112.6

Sampling Error

Sampling error (or variability) is the statistical error that occurs because a sample was surveyed rather than the entire population. Data from sample surveys are only estimates of what a complete count would have shown, and the sampling error for a survey provides a measure of the reliability of survey results. Together, the sample estimate and the standard error for the survey are used to construct a confidence interval. That is, the survey response and the measure of sampling error provide a measure of the accuracy of the data that is expressed in terms of the range, which would include the average result of all possible samples with a known probability. Surveys will generally include information on sampling error as part of the footnotes or appendixes.

Farm Labor

The estimates of agricultural labor published in *Farm Labor* are based on multiple-frame probability surveys. Information on standard error for these surveys is given in the section on source and reliability of estimates. According to the information provided, the true value for the population is expected to be within the range of two standard errors below to two standard errors above the survey indication nineteen times out of twenty. For example, the standard error for the number of hired workers at the regional level, as published in *Farm Labor*, is between 10 and 20 percent. The survey indication for the number of workers on farms in the Northeast I Region (the states of Connecticut, Maine, Massachusetts, New Hampshire, New York, Rhode Island, and Vermont) for the survey week of April 8 to 14, 1990, was 102,000. On the basis of a standard error of 20 percent, the true value can be expected to lie between 81,600 and 122,400 nineteen out of twenty times.

Current Population Survey

The 1989 publication *Labor Force Status and Other Characteristics of Persons with a Work Disability: 1981 to 1988 (Current Population Reports: Series*

P-23, No. 160) is based largely on the CPS conducted each March. It is intended to provide a reasonably consistent set of time series data on the labor force activity and earnings of persons with a work disability. The appendixes provide information on methodology and procedures employed in the survey, including the source and accuracy of the estimates contained in the report.

There are two formulas provided for the calculation of the standard error of an estimated number (s_x). Formula one is given as

$$s_x = fs$$

where f is a factor provided in the appendixes for specific characteristics of the population and s is the standard error of the estimate based on the size of the estimate as provided in the appendixes. Formula two is given as

$$s_x = \sqrt{ax^2 + bx}$$

where x is the size of the estimate and a and b are the parameters associated with the particular type of data for which the confidence level is being calculated. The Census Bureau states that formula two will provide more accurate results. The following illustration is provided. The survey estimates that there were 3,791,000 males with a severe work disability in 1988. Using formula one, the tables provide the following data for the calculation of the standard error: $f = .9$ and $s = 91,000$. The standard error is, then, equal to .9 times 91,000, or 81,900. Using formula two, the tables provide the following data: $a = -.000023$ and $b = 2,013$, and the standard error equals 85,000. The appendixes also state that the 90 percent confidence interval for the CPS is from 1.6 standard errors above to 1.6 standard errors below the survey estimate. That is, if all possible samples were surveyed under essentially the same general conditions, approximately 90 percent of all samples would yield an average result that falls within 1.6 standard errors above the estimate and 1.6 standard errors below the estimate. Using the more accurate estimate of standard error (85,000 from formula two), the 90 percent confidence interval is from 3,655,000 to 3,927,000. That is, 90 percent of the time the average estimate derived from all possible samples lies within the range of 3,655,000 and 3,927,000.

Cost of Living Index

The ACCRA publishes an index known as the ACCRA Cost of Living Index. The index measures the relative differences in the cost of living among a number of urban areas at a specific point in time. The City Composite Index is based on the prices of a number of goods and services appropriate for a midmanagement standard of living and is expressed

Table 8-5. ACCRA Cost of Living Index, All-Items Index, U.S. City Average = 100, 4th Quarter 1982

City	Index
Birmingham, Ala.	102.5
Mobile, Ala.	98.7
Montgomery, Ala.	100.1
Little Rock, Ark.	103.0
Blythe, Calif.	99.5
Indio, Calif.	101.8
Riverside, Calif.	100.9
Waterbury, Conn.	103.0
Lakeland, Fla.	98.5
Miami, Fla.	99.0
Orlando, Fla.	102.6
Augusta, Ga.	97.1
Dalton, Ga.	98.1
Boise, Idaho	100.5

Source: American Chamber of Commerce Researchers Association, *Inter-city Cost of Living Index*, 4th qtr., 1982 (Louisville, Ky.: ACCRA).

as the U.S. city average = 100. User documentation notes that differences of 3 percent or less in the Composite Index are not significant. In other words, the index is considered to be accurate plus or minus three points. Table 8-5 provides the ACCRA Cost of Living Index, All-Items Index, select cities for the fourth quarter of 1982. The index for Augusta, Georgia, is 97.1, and the index for Blythe, California, is 99.5. Despite the fact that Blythe's index is higher than Augusta's, it is not possible to determine which city has the higher cost of living for the quarter. The true value of the index for Augusta could be as low as 94.1 and as high as 100.1; while the index for Blythe could range from 96.5 to 102.5. On the other hand, at 97.1 Augusta is likely to be approximately 6 percent less expensive than Little Rock, Arkansas, at 103.0.

Questionnaire Design

Questionnaire design has an important impact on survey results. What questions are asked, how they are worded, and how the survey was conducted all have an impact on survey responses. Conversely, when interpreting data obtained by questionnaire, it is important to keep in mind how the survey instrument was designed and implemented.

For example, table one of the *1970 Census Subject Report PC(2)-6D: Journey to Work* shows the number of people living in the San Francisco SMSA and working in various places around the country (see Table 8-6). The data appear to reflect that in 1980, eighty-one people in

San Francisco commuted to Hawaii and forty-three to Vietnam by car. These strange data could be attributable to respondent errors; however, another possible explanation is questionnaire design. Reference to the questionnaire reveals that the question upon which the table was based was worded: "Where did you work last week?" Thus, responses from people who moved during the week prior to the census or who were on a business trip would not reflect what is normally considered commuting to work. An analogous explanation might account for people who reported that they commuted to work by subway and yet live in areas where no subway system exists.

Indexing

Indexing is a common statistical technique that provides a convenient and straightforward method for making comparisons. An index number is a percentage of some base selected to serve as the standard for comparisons. Most notable among the economic indexes are the CPI, the PPI, and the Index of Industrial Production (IIP). Typically, though not always, indexes are used to facilitate comparison over time. In such cases, an index is constructed based on the level of activity in a given period or year and the base is defined as being equal to 100. Index numbers for periods either before or after that base year are represented as a pecentage of the base. For example, if an index is set at 1990 = 100 and the level of activity for the measure in question is double the 1990 level in 1991, then the index for 1991 equals 200. A key factor governing the appropriate use of an index is the base used in the construction of that index.

Consumer Price Index

The CPI measures the average change in prices paid by urban consumers for a fixed market basket of goods and services. There is an entire family of consumer price indexes produced by the BLS designed to measure change for various segments of the urban population, geographic areas, or components of the market basket. In order to reflect change in price levels, the base of the CPI is a specific point or period of time. Currently, the base for the CPI is 1982–84 = 100.

The main index of consumer prices is the Consumer Price Index for All Urban Consumers, U.S. City Average. Table 8-7 provides sample data for the CPI-U. The table shows the relative price levels for the average of all U.S. cities for the period 1954–1989 (with 1982–84 as the base) for all items in the CPI market basket for all urban consumers. For example, with an index of 51.9, average consumer prices for all urban consumers

Table 8-6. Place of Work of Workers Residing in the San Francisco-Oakland (Calif.) SMSA, Means of Transportation, 1970

San Francisco-Oakland (Calif.), SMSA	All means	Private automobile, driver or passenger
Living in SMSA	1,252,710	924,651
Working in SMSA	1,083,751	798,277
Working outside SMSA	44,537	39,027
Arizona	151	110
California	40,043	36,755
Fresno County	225	162
Kern County	181	166
Los Angeles County	1,358	1,000
Monterey County	270	216
Napa County	409	349
Orange County	458	404
Placer County	168	128
Sacramento County	522	451
San Bernardino County	131	80
San Diego County	236	119
San Joaquin County	634	556
Santa Barbara County	116	62
Santa Clara County	29,153	27,572
Santa Cruz County	210	121
Solano County	3,550	3,402
Sonoma County	1,089	971
Stanislaus County	132	123
Ventura County	177	136
Yolo County	208	150
Connecticut	133	100
Florida	164	85
Hawaii	165	81
Illinois	145	67
Massachusetts	137	72
Nevada	141	81
New Jersey	118	67
New York	362	177
Oregon	175	115
Washington	265	167
Vietnam	144	43
Abroad, not reported	669	254

Source: U.S. Bureau of the Census, *1970 Census of Population Subject Reports: Journey to Work (PC(2)-6D)* (Washington, D.C.: U.S. Government Printing Office, 1973), p.195–96.

in 1974 were approximately half the 1982–84 level. In contrast, Table 8-8 provides data on the price levels for all items in the CPI market basket for select local areas in the United States for the period October 1989 to January 1990. The base remains 1982–84 = 100. Therefore, these indexes provide a basis for comparisons of price levels for specific places over the time period, not comparisons of price levels from place to place.

Table 8-7. Consumer Price Index for All Urban Consumers, U.S. City Average, 1982–84 = 100

Year/Month	All items	Year/Month	All items
1954, Dec.	26.7	1972, Dec.	42.5
1955, Dec.	26.8	1973, Dec.	46.2
1956, Dec.	27.6	1974, Dec.	51.9
1957, Dec.	28.4	1975, Dec.	55.5
1958, Dec.	28.9	1976, Dec.	58.2
1959, Dec.	29.4	1977, Dec.	62.1
1960, Dec.	29.8	1978, Dec.	67.7
1961, Dec.	30.0	1979, Dec.	76.7
1962, Dec.	30.4	1980, Dec.	86.3
1963, Dec.	30.9	1981, Dec.	94.0
1964, Dec.	31.2	1982, Dec.	97.6
1965, Dec.	31.8	1983, Dec.	101.3
1966, Dec.	32.9	1984, Dec.	105.3
1967, Dec.	33.9	1985, Dec.	109.3
1968, Dec.	35.5	1986, Dec.	110.5
1969, Dec.	37.7	1987, Dec.	115.4
1970, Dec.	39.8	1988, Dec.	120.5
1971, Dec.	41.1	1989, Dec.	126.1

Source: U.S. Bureau of Labor Statistics, *CPI Detailed Report* (January 1990).

For example, on the basis of the CPI-U, Selected Areas, it is possible to determine that price levels in Los Angeles did not rise appreciably from October to November 1989; however, it is not possible to determine that prices for Los Angeles for October 1989 were at the same level as prices for Philadelphia, or to make any comparisons of price levels from city to city on the basis of the CPI.

Cost of Living Index

Unlike the CPI-U, Selected Areas, the ACCRA Cost of Living Index allows for geographic comparisons of cost of living or price levels. Data for selected cities for the 100% Composite Index are given in Table 8-9. These data cover the second quarter of 1989 through the second quarter

Table 8-8. Consumer Price Index, Selected Areas, All-Items Index, October 1989–January 1990, 1982–84 = 100

Selected Local Areas	10/1989	11/1989	12/1989	1/1990
Chicago-Gary-Lake County, Ill.-Ind.-Wis.	126.8	126.7	126.5	128.1
Los Angeles-Anaheim-Riverside, Calif.	130.0	130.0	130.6	132.1
N.Y.-Northern N.J.-Long Island, N.Y.-N.J.-Conn.	132.8	133.2	133.3	135.1
Philadelphia-Wilmington-Trenton, Pa.-N.J.-Del.-Md.	130.5	130.1	129.9	131.2
San Francisco-Oakland-San Jose, Calif.	127.5	127.2	127.4	128.5

Source: U.S. Bureau of Labor Statistics, *CPI Detailed Report* (January 1990).

Table 8-9. ACCRA Cost of Living Index, 100% Composite Index,
U.S. Average = 100

Selected local areas	II 1989	III 1989	IV 1989	I 1989	II 1990
Los Angeles County, Calif.	—	126.5	129.2	127.4	124.1
Philadelphia, Pa.	127.2	127.2	129.2	127.5	127.8
Riverside City, Calif.	108.3	106.7	107.3	112.6	112.2
San Jose, Calif.	—	—	129.9	129.3	—
Wilmington, Del.	119.1	117.7	120.4	117.4	117.1

Source: American Chamber of Commerce Researchers Association, *Cost of Living Index*, 2nd qtr. 1989,
1st qtr. 1990 (Louisville, Ky.: ACCRA).
— data not provided

of 1990. Unlike the CPI data for local areas provided in Table 8-8, the
ACCRA data allow comparisons of costs in various geographic areas. On
the basis of the data given, it is possible to determine that costs in the
fourth quarter of 1989 were appreciably higher in Los Angeles County
than in Riverside. However, because this index uses as its base the average
cost for participating cities at a specific point in time, it is not possible to
draw conclusions about changes in costs over time. For example, the data
given for San Jose do not show that costs remained relatively constant
there from the fourth quarter of 1989 to the first quarter of 1990. This
index reflects only that costs in San Jose maintained essentially the same
relationship to the average for participating cities for those two quarters.

Annual Comparisons

There are several methods for evaluating changes in the economy from
year to year. Different methods for making annual comparisons will yield
different results. For example, annual changes may be evaluated by comparing levels at the close of the year (fourth quarter or December data)
for each year. This type of comparison does not take into account any
large swings in data for the given period and, for this reason, may distort the view of annual change. Another approach to measuring changes
from year to year is to compare annual averages. This measure smooths
out the effect of short-term variations in the data over the course of the
year and provides a more complete picture of activity than comparing a
single period.

Employment and Unemployment

Table 8-10 provides employment and unemployment data for the civilian noninstitutional population in 1988 and 1989. Both seasonally
adjusted and unadjusted data for December are given, as are annual

Table 8-10. Employment Status of the Civilian Noninstitutional Population, 1988–1989 (in thousands)

Month/Year	Employed	Unemployed
Monthly data, seasonally adjusted:		
Dec. 1988	116,141	6,509
Dec. 1989	117,888	6,658
Change 1988 to 1989	1,747	149
Monthly data, not adjusted:		
Dec. 1988	115,978	6,142
Dec. 1989	117,968	6,300
Change 1988 to 1989	1,990	158
Annual averages:		
1988	114,968	6,701
1989	117,342	6,528
Change 1988 to 1989	2,374	−173

Source: U.S. Bureau of Labor Statistics, *Employment and Earnings* (January 1989 and January 1990).

averages for both years. Although the figures themselves vary for seasonally adjusted and unadjusted data, the change from 1988 to 1989 is very close for both employment and unemployment series. However, the annual average data reflect a significantly different trend. While approximately 1,990,000 more individuals were employed in December 1989 than in December 1988, the change in the annual average was nearly 2,400,000. Likewise, approximately 150,000 *more* persons were unemployed in December 1989 than in December 1988 (whether data are seasonally adjusted or unadjusted); however, using annual averages, approximately 175,000 *fewer* persons were unemployed in 1989 than in 1988.

Seasonal Adjustment

Many data series are subject to seasonal variation. For example, employment data may jump in June and July due to the number of graduates who join the work force, or in December due to short-term employment for the Christmas season. Likewise, retail sales jump in November and December due to holiday gift giving. Air travel also peaks predictably at several times during the year due to holidays and summer vacations. Statistical procedures have been developed that attempt to remove this seasonal influence from time series data. When such procedures have been employed to correct the data for seasonal factors, data series are referred to as seasonally adjusted. Data may also be expressed as seasonally adjusted at annual rates, which reflects what the yearly movement of the

Table 8-11. Money Supply M1, 1988–1989 (billions of dollars)

Date	Seasonally adjusted	Unadjusted
Jan. 1988	757.50	768.30
Feb. 1988	759.40	745.70
Mar. 1988	763.00	752.80
Apr. 1988	770.10	779.20
May 1988	773.10	764.70
June 1988	778.90	779.90
July 1988	783.40	786.90
Aug. 1988	784.40	782.40
Sept. 1988	784.80	781.10
Oct. 1988	785.10	782.20
Nov. 1988	786.00	788.30
Dec. 1988	787.50	804.50
Jan. 1989	785.80	793.50
Feb. 1989	786.70	773.00
Mar. 1989	785.50	775.90
Apr. 1989	782.10	791.60
May 1989	776.20	767.70
June 1989	773.70	774.40
July 1989	779.10	782.30
Aug. 1989	780.40	778.10
Sept. 1989	782.90	779.10
Oct. 1989	788.10	785.00
Nov. 1989	789.40	791.70
Dec. 1989	794.80	812.10

Source: Citibase: Citibank economic database, machine-readable datafile (New York: Citibank, 1946–).

measure would be if the same rate of change (adjusted for seasonality) were to continue over the entire year.

Money Stock

Table 8-11 provides both seasonally adjusted and unadjusted data for the U.S. money supply measure M1. M1 equals the sum of currency, travelers checks, demand deposits, and other checkable deposits. Data are presented for the period 1959 to 1989. Figure 8-1 graphically demonstrates the difference in the trends reflected by the data, depending on whether the data have been recalculated to remove any fluctuation due to seasonal influences. Seasonal adjustment smooths out the peaks in December, January, and March, as well as the troughs in February and May.

Consumer Price Index for Energy

In addition to the aggregate consumer price indexes, the BLS calculates indexes for segments of the urban population, geographic areas, and

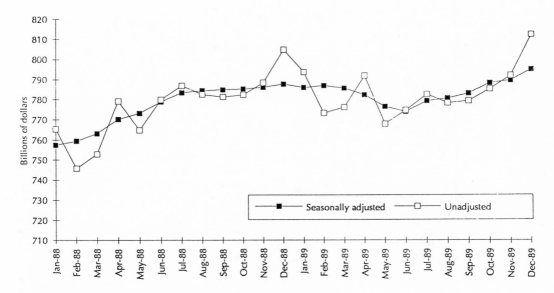

Figure 8-1. Money Supply M1, seasonally adjusted

components of the CPI market basket. The market basket components for which special indexes are calculated include food, housing, fuel, and transportation. One special index that is subject to seasonal influences is the Consumer Price Index for Energy. Table 8-12 provides both seasonally adjusted and unadjusted data for the CPI-U for Energy. Figure 8-2 plots data series and demonstrates the difference that seasonal adjustment makes.

Table 8-12. CPI-U for Energy, 1988 (1967 = 100)

Date	CPI-U—Energy, seasonally adjusted	CPI-U—Energy, unadjusted
Jan. 1988	88.700	87.400
Feb. 1988	88.700	87.000
Mar. 198	88.200	86.500
Apr. 1988	88.400	87.300
May 1988	88.400	88.700
June 1988	88.400	91.000
July 1988	88.800	91.400
Aug. 1988	89.300	92.300
Sept. 1988	89.300	91.900
Oct. 1988	89.400	89.900
Nov. 1988	89.500	88.900
Dec. 1988	89.500	88.700

Source: Citibase: Citibank economic database, machine-readable datafile (New York: Citibank, 1946–).

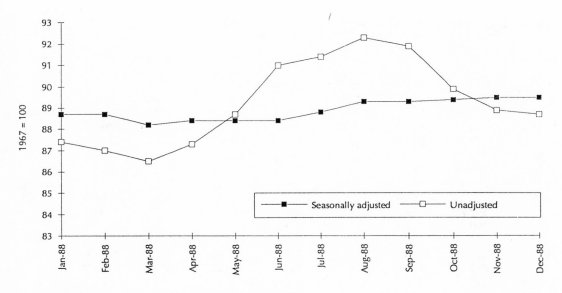

Figure 8-2. CPI-U for Energy, seasonally adjusted

Current and Constant Dollar Estimates

As with seasonality, the comparability of many time series is affected by changes in the value of the dollar. In the same way that seasonal adjustment procedures have been developed to remove seasonal influences, procedures also exist that adjust data for changes in price levels or inflation. Adjusted data are frequently referred to as constant dollar estimates.

Gross National Product

Table 8-13 provides both current and constant (or inflation-adjusted) estimates for the GNP for the period 1947 through 1989. Figure 8-3 demonstrates the impact of inflation adjustment on the data series.

Variant Sources

As the first seven chapters of this book demonstrate, there are frequently multiple sources of data for a given economic process. For example, both the BEA and the Federal Reserve collect and disseminate information on U.S. production. Different data producers may compile data on a given topic, using different methodologies and underlying definitions to suit their differing purposes. Therefore, different data sources may be consulted for data on a given topic with very different results.

Table 8-13. Gross National Product in Current and Constant (1982) Dollars, 1947–1989

Year. qtr.	Current dollars	Constant 1982 $	Year. qtr.	Current dollars	Constant 1982 $	Year. qtr.	Current dollars	Constant 1982 $
1947.1	227.5	1056.5	1958.3	461.0	1550.0	1970.1	994.2	2408.6
1947.2	231.5	1063.2	1958.4	474.2	1586.7	1970.2	1008.9	2406.5
1947.3	235.9	1067.1	1959.1	485.1	1606.4	1970.3	1027.9	2435.8
1947.4	246.1	1080.0	1959.2	497.8	1637.0	1970.4	1030.9	2413.8
1948.1	252.4	1086.8	1959.3	498.0	1629.5	1971.1	1075.2	2478.6
1948.2	259.7	1106.1	1959.4	502.4	1643.4	1971.2	1094.3	2478.4
1948.3	266.6	1116.3	1960.1	516.1	1671.6	1971.3	1113.9	2491.1
1948.4	267.9	1125.5	1960.2	514.5	1666.8	1971.4	1127.3	2491.0
1949.1	262.7	1112.4	1960.3	517.7	1668.4	1972.1	1166.5	2545.6
1949.2	259.2	1105.9	1960.4	513.0	1654.1	1972.2	1197.2	2595.1
1949.3	260.9	1114.3	1961.1	517.4	1671.3	1972.3	1223.9	2622.1
1949.4	258.6	1103.3	1961.2	527.9	1692.1	1972.4	1263.5	2671.3
1950.1	269.3	1148.2	1961.3	538.5	1716.3	1973.1	1311.6	2734.0
1950.2	278.9	1181.0	1961.4	551.5	1754.9	1973.2	1342.9	2741.0
1950.3	296.7	1225.3	1962.1	564.4	1777.9	1973.3	1369.4	2738.3
1950.4	308.1	1260.2	1962.2	572.2	1796.4	1973.4	1413.3	2762.8
1951.1	322.9	1286.6	1962.3	579.2	1813.1	1974.1	1426.2	2747.4
1951.2	330.9	1320.4	1962.4	582.8	1810.1	1974.2	1459.1	2755.2
1951.3	337.7	1349.8	1963.1	592.1	1834.6	1974.3	1489.1	2719.3
1951.4	342.1	1356.0	1963.2	600.3	1860.0	1974.4	1516.8	2695.4
1952.1	345.2	1369.2	1963.3	613.1	1892.5	1975.1	1524.6	2642.7
1952.2	345.7	1365.9	1963.4	622.1	1906.1	1975.2	1563.5	2669.6
1952.3	351.6	1378.2	1964.1	636.9	1948.7	1975.3	1627.4	2714.9
1952.4	364.0	1406.8	1964.2	645.6	1965.4	1975.4	1678.2	2752.7
1953.1	370.7	1431.4	1964.3	656.0	1985.2	1976.1	1730.9	2804.4
1953.2	374.1	1444.9	1964.4	660.6	1993.7	1976.2	1761.8	2816.9
1953.3	373.3	1438.2	1965.1	682.7	2036.9	1976.3	1794.7	2828.6
1953.4	368.2	1426.6	1965.2	695.0	2066.4	1976.4	1843.7	2856.8
1954.1	367.9	1406.8	1965.3	710.7	2099.3	1977.1	1899.1	2896.0
1954.2	368.1	1401.2	1965.4	732.0	2147.6	1977.2	1968.9	2942.7
1954.3	372.8	1418.0	1966.1	754.8	2190.1	1977.3	2031.6	3001.8
1954.4	381.2	1438.8	1966.2	764.6	2195.8	1977.4	2062.4	2994.1
1955.1	394.0	1469.6	1966.3	777.7	2218.3	1978.1	2111.4	3020.5
1955.2	402.3	1485.7	1966.4	790.9	2229.2	1978.2	2230.3	3115.9
1955.3	410.5	1505.5	1967.1	799.7	2241.8	1978.3	2289.5	3142.6
1955.4	416.9	1518.7	1967.2	805.9	2255.2	1978.4	2367.6	3181.6
1956.1	419.5	1515.7	1967.3	822.9	2287.7	1979.1	2420.5	3181.7
1956.2	425.1	1522.6	1967.4	837.1	2300.6	1979.2	2474.5	3178.7
1956.3	429.9	1523.7	1968.1	862.9	2327.3	1979.3	2546.1	3207.4
1956.4	438.3	1540.6	1968.2	886.7	2366.9	1979.4	2591.5	3201.3
1957.1	447.3	1553.3	1968.3	903.6	2385.3	1980.1	2673.0	3233.4
1957.2	449.4	1552.4	1968.4	917.4	2383.0	1980.2	2672.2	3157.0
1957.3	456.5	1561.5	1969.1	941.3	2416.5	1980.3	2734.0	3159.1
1957.4	450.9	1537.3	1969.2	955.6	2419.8	1980.4	2848.6	3199.2
1958.1	443.9	1506.1	1969.3	975.4	2433.2	1981.1	2978.8	3261.1
1958.2	447.9	1514.2	1969.4	983.5	2423.5	1981.2	3017.7	3250.2

Year. qtr.	Current dollars	Constant 1982 $	Year. qtr.	Current dollars	Constant 1982 $	Year. qtr.	Current dollars	Constant 1982 $
1981.3	3099.6	3264.6	1984.3	3807.9	3520.6	1987.3	4566.6	3872.8
1981.4	3114.4	3219.0	1984.4	3851.8	3535.2	1987.4	4665.8	3935.6
1982.1	3112.6	3170.4	1985.1	3925.6	3577.5	1988.1	4739.8	3974.8
1982.2	3159.5	3179.9	1985.2	3979.0	3599.2	1988.2	4838.5	4010.7
1982.3	3179.4	3145.5	1985.3	4047.0	3635.8	1988.3	4926.9	4042.7
1982.4	3212.5	3159.3	1985.4	4107.9	3662.4	1988.4	5017.3	4069.4
1983.1	3265.8	3186.6	1986.1	4181.3	3721.1	1989.1	5113.1	4106.8
1983.2	3367.4	3258.3	1986.2	4194.7	3704.6	1989.2	5201.7	4132.5
1983.3	3443.9	3306.4	1986.3	4253.3	3712.4	1989.3	5281.0	4162.9
1983.4	3545.8	3365.1	1986.4	4297.3	3733.6	1989.4	5340.2	4174.1
1984.1	3674.9	3451.7	1987.1	4388.8	3783.0			
1984.2	3754.2	3498.0	1987.2	4475.9	3823.5			

Source: Citibase: Citibank economic database, machine-readable datafile (New York: Citibank, 1946–).

Government Finance

As outlined in chapter 7, several sources within the federal government collect data on government finance. The OMB is responsible for the budget itself, while the Bureau of the Census compiles data on federal finance that are comparable to its data on finance for other levels of government. In addition, annual financial data may be based on a fiscal-year or calendar-year basis. As Table 8-14 demonstrates, the data vary significantly depending on the choice of source and fiscal- or calendar-year data. For example, federal receipts on the NIPA basis for fiscal year

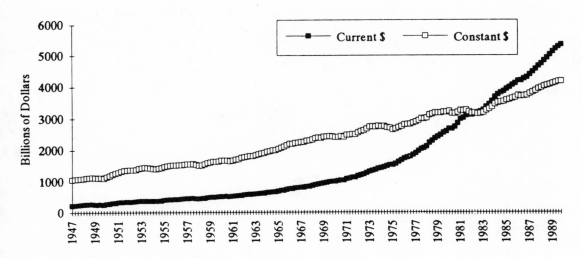

Figure 8-3. Gross National Product, current and constant dollar estimates

Table 8-14. Total Federal Receipts and Outlays, 1977-1989 (billions of dollars)

	U.S. Budget (fiscal year)	NIPA Basis (fiscal year)	NIPA Basis (calendar year)
Receipts:			
1985	734.1	776.8	788.7
1986	769.1	815.2	827.9
1987	854.1	899.4	913.8
1988	909.0	957.6	972.4
1989	990.7	1,041.9	1,052.9
Outlays:			
1985	946.3	962.3	985.6
1986	990.3	1,028.0	1,034.8
1987	1,003.8	1,060.0	1,071.9
1988	1,064.0	1,101.8	1,114.2
1989	1,142.6	1,172.2	1,187.2

Source: Council of Economic Advisors, *Economic Indicators* (September 1990).

1987 were $899.4 billion. For calendar year 1987, the NIPA estimate of federal receipts was $913.8 billion. According to the budget itself, federal receipts for fiscal year 1987 were only $854.1 billion.

International Debt

Data on U.S. imports and exports can be obtained from several sources. As outlined in chapter 6, the Census Bureau tracks merchandise imports and exports. The BEA also calculates imports and exports of goods and services as part of the NIPAs and the international transactions accounts (see Figures 8-4 and 8-5). Each source varies in its definitions and methodology. Tables 8-15 and 8-16 provide BEA data on exports and imports of goods and services. BEA estimates are provided from the international transactions accounts, as well as from the Foreign Transactions Account of the NIPAs. Also provided is the percentage difference between the two accounts.

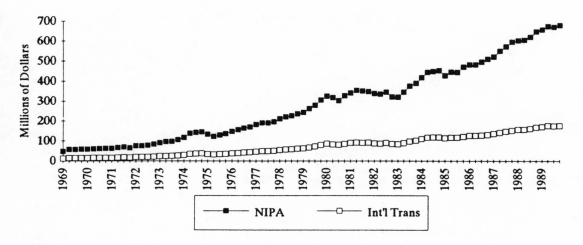

Figure 8-4. Exports of Goods and Services, variant sources

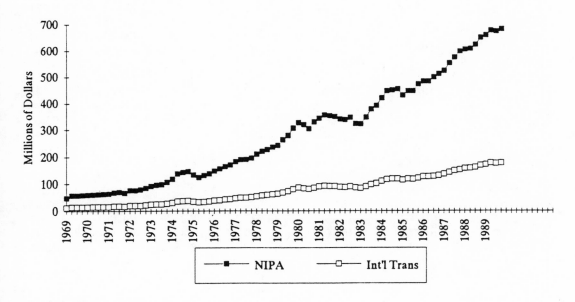

Figure 8-5. Imports of Goods and Services, variant sources

Table 8-15. Exports of Goods and Services in Millions of Dollars, 1969–1989

Year. qtr.	Foreign trans. (NIPA)	Int'l. trans.	Year. qtr.	Foreign trans. (NIPA)	Int'l. trans.
1969.1	52.40	12.428	1979.3	301.00	74.405
1969.2	61.80	14.753	1979.4	320.60	79.715
1969.3	62.40	14.871	1980.1	346.50	84.969
1969.4	64.90	15.469	1980.2	348.40	82.733
1970.1	66.70	15.902	1980.3	350.10	86.126
1970.2	69.90	16.68	1980.4	358.90	88.659
1970.3	69.40	16.532	1981.1	380.70	94.581
1970.4	69.60	16.561	1981.2	383.40	95.446
1971.1	71.80	17.097	1981.3	382.30	94.759
1971.2	72.60	17.288	1981.4	384.80	93.913
1971.3	75.30	17.943	1982.1	373.00	90.619
1971.4	69.70	16.508	1982.2	378.90	91.88
1972.1	77.80	18.512	1982.3	359.90	88.269
1972.2	77.60	18.445	1982.4	335.90	81.361
1972.3	81.90	19.498	1983.1	343.60	82.257
1972.4	88.20	21.039	1983.2	344.10	82.602
1973.1	100.10	23.958	1983.3	357.70	86.311
1973.2	109.40	26.259	1983.4	364.70	86.213
1973.3	118.70	28.544	1984.1	374.30	91.913
1973.4	128.30	31.479	1984.2	383.20	92.436
1974.1	141.70	34.293	1984.3	390.80	94.014
1974.2	151.50	36.73	1984.4	385.70	92.733
1974.3	152.90	37.033	1985.1	376.80	90.532
1974.4	159.90	38.609	1985.2	372.60	92.932
1975.1	162.00	39.26	1985.3	365.10	93.947
1975.2	155.40	37.474	1985.4	369.20	93.8
1975.3	159.00	38.293	1986.1	395.50	97.413
1975.4	168.90	40.705	1986.2	390.70	98.115
1976.1	170.60	41.112	1986.3	397.30	98.322
1976.2	175.10	42.2	1986.4	402.40	98.109
1976.3	180.50	43.644	1987.1	416.50	104.315
1976.4	184.80	44.674	1987.2	437.40	105.694
1977.1	186.30	44.837	1987.3	458.00	110.922
1977.2	194.00	46.699	1987.4	482.60	125.211
1977.3	195.90	47.049	1988.1	521.60	127.81
1977.4	190.30	45.692	1988.2	532.50	126.8
1978.1	203.80	49.096	1988.3	556.80	131.573
1978.2	222.10	54.086	1988.4	579.70	143.626
1978.3	233.20	55.94	1989.1	605.60	146.826
1978.4	250.90	60.873	1989.2	626.10	151.131
1979.1	265.20	64.693	1989.3	628.50	150.653
1979.2	278.10	67.983	1989.4	643.50	154.558

Source: Citibase: Citibank economic database, machine-readable datafile (New York: Citibank, 1946–).

Table 8-16. Imports of Goods and Services in Millions of Dollars, 1969–1989

Year. qtr.	Foreign trans. (NIPA)	Int'l. trans.	Year. qtr.	Foreign trans. (NIPA)	Int'l. trans.
1969.1	47.20	11.622	1979.3	279.20	72.605
1969.2	56.60	13.978	1979.4	305.20	78.921
1969.3	57.00	14.072	1980.1	325.80	85.491
1969.4	58.10	14.329	1980.2	318.30	82.32
1970.1	58.60	14.458	1980.3	303.30	80.563
1970.2	60.10	14.861	1980.4	328.10	84.648
1970.3	61.00	15.141	1981.1	341.90	89.808
1970.4	62.20	15.443	1981.2	354.40	91.724
1971.1	62.40	15.551	1981.3	351.40	90.363
1971.2	67.00	16.764	1981.4	347.90	90.993
1971.3	69.30	17.46	1982.1	338.40	88.001
1971.4	65.70	16.639	1982.2	336.80	86.702
1972.1	75.60	19.153	1982.3	345.40	89.941
1972.2	75.40	19.105	1982.4	321.90	85.291
1972.3	78.10	19.767	1983.1	320.90	83.721
1972.4	83.70	21.212	1983.2	346.20	89.689
1973.1	90.60	23.0	1983.3	376.90	97.384
1973.2	95.50	24.301	1983.4	390.50	101.102
1973.3	97.60	24.841	1984.1	420.00	109.996
1973.4	105.70	26.855	1984.2	446.10	116.095
1974.1	116.80	29.643	1984.3	450.10	118.335
1974.2	136.90	34.71	1984.4	453.60	118.391
1974.3	142.20	36.004	1985.1	429.90	113.508
1974.4	145.10	36.918	1985.2	446.90	117.397
1975.1	132.80	33.797	1985.3	446.20	116.922
1975.2	122.70	31.284	1985.4	472.40	120.644
1975.3	129.70	33.078	1986.1	482.70	125.693
1975.4	136.00	34.588	1986.2	483.40	125.768
1976.1	147.00	37.464	1986.3	498.00	127.532
1976.2	155.10	39.494	1986.4	511.30	130.439
1976.3	163.40	41.737	1987.1	522.50	135.505
1976.4	170.10	43.416	1987.2	551.80	141.249
1977.1	182.30	46.36	1987.3	573.40	147.609
1977.2	189.80	48.401	1987.4	597.20	151.266
1977.3	190.60	48.511	1988.1	604.30	156.492
1977.4	196.20	50.495	1988.2	607.50	157.386
1978.1	210.40	54.028	1988.3	623.00	160.537
1978.2	220.70	56.525	1988.4	650.50	167.285
1978.3	226.40	58.565	1989.1	659.60	170.375
1978.4	236.00	60.752	1989.2	676.60	176.774
1979.1	242.60	62.72	1989.3	673.60	174.714
1979.2	262.90	67.414	1989.4	682.30	176.619

Source: Citibase: Citibank economic database, machine-readable datafile (New York: Citibank, 1946–).

Availability of Machine-Readable Versions of Statistical Data

This appendix provides information on the availability of machine-readable versions of the statistical data described in this volume. As with the references to print materials in the body of the work, only the official government sources of data are included. However, many of the data series are available in commercial products, such as Citibase and Slater Hall's machine-readable products.

Board of Governors of the Federal Reserve System

Index of Industrial Production (chapter 5)

The IIP is available on computer tape from the National Technical Information Service (5285 Port Royal Road, Springfield, VA 22161). The tape provides monthly data from 1954 to the present. The datafile includes 235 individual series providing information for various industrial groupings. Data are provided both seasonally adjusted and unadjusted. As of early 1991, the data were priced at $210 for one cumulative tape.

Money Supply (chapter 8)

The Federal Reserve Board produces a Money Stock Tape that covers the period 1959 to 1984. This tape contains aggregate money stock data, as well as component measures. Monthly data are provided for the period 1959 to 1984, and weekly data are provided for the period 1975 to 1984. As of early 1991, the Money Stock Tape was $210 from the National Technical Information Service (5285 Port Royal Road, Springfield, VA 22161).

U.S. Bureau of Economic Analysis

Input-Output Accounts (chapter 5)

The complete 1977 Benchmark 85—Industry Input-Output Tables are available on computer tape and floppy diskette. The annual tables based on the 1977 benchmark are also available in machine-readable form. There are five tables in both the benchmark and the annual accounts: use table, make table, commodity-by-industry direct requirements table, commodity-by-commodity total requirements table, and industry-by-commodity total requirements table. Pricing for either the benchmark or the annual tables is the same. The computer tape version is $100. The diskette version is $40.

National Income and Product Accounts (chapters 4, 5, 6, 7, and 8)

Historic data for the NIPAs tables are available for $100 on diskette or computer tape. Monthly updates are available on diskette only for $200 per year.

U.S. Economic Indicators and Indexes (chapter 3)

Historic data for the economic indicators are available on diskette for $40. Current data are $200 per year on floppy diskette.

In addition to its computer tape and diskette products, the BEA maintains the Electronic Bulletin Board (EBB). This online system contains most BEA statistical releases. The EBB is available through the National Technical Information Service (5285 Port Royal Road, Springfield, VA 22161). Information on the system is available from the U.S. Commerce Department's Office of Business Analysis (14th Street between Constitution Avenue and E Street NW, Washington, DC 20230).

U.S. Bureau of Labor Statistics

Consumer Price Index (chapters 4 and 8)

U.S. city averages for the CPI-U and CPI-W are available for 355 consumer items and groups of items on a single computer tape. In addition, many of the series have been seasonally adjusted. Area indexes for both populations are available for twenty-seven urban areas. For each area, indexes are available for sixty items or groups of items. These data are also available from the BLS on floppy diskette.

Current Population Survey (chapters 1, 2, and 8)

See U.S. Bureau of the Census—Current Population Survey.

Industry Employment, Hours and Earnings (chapters 2 and 8)

There are two separate series available: one containing national data; one containing state and area data. In the national file, nearly 1,500 monthly employment series are available for all employees, women, and production or nonsupervisory workers. About 11,700 data series are available for production workers' weekly earnings, average hourly earnings, average weekly hours, and—in manufacturing—average weekly overtime. Similar data are available in the state and area files, with data disaggregated for states and major labor areas (largely MSAs). Employment data are also available on floppy diskette.

Producer Price Index (chapter 4)

Monthly indexes are provided on computer tape for about 3,200 individual commodities and commodity groups. Indexes are also available by stage of processing and durability of product. These data are also available on floppy diskette.

Many BLS statistical data series are available in the online Electronic News Release Service. The service is available to the public through Electronic Data Systems Corporation (5615 Fishers Lane, Rockville, MD 20852).

Prices vary from product to product, however. BLS data on computer tape average approximately $100 per series, with most series fitting on a single reel of tape at 6,250 bpi. Prices for data on diskette also vary depending on the number of diskettes required. Single diskettes are $35; annual subscriptions vary from approximately $100 to $300.

U.S. Bureau of the Census

Census of Population and Housing (chapters 1, 2, and 8)

Data from the 1990 census will be released as Summary Tape Files (STFs) and Public Use Microdata files (PUMs). The STFs provide data with greater subject and geographic detail than is feasible or desirable in print. The PUMs provide users with the flexibility to produce customized tabulations.

Summary Tape Files: Four STFs are planned for the 1990 census. These files are comparable in subject content and coverage to STFs 1 through 4 for the 1980 census. The source data for STF 1 will be the same as for the CPH-1, CPH-2, and CPH-4 printed reports. The source data for STF 2 will be the same as for the CPH-3, CP-1, and CH-1 printed reports. STF 3 will be based on the same data as are the CPH-4 and CPH-5 printed reports. STF 4 will be based on the same data as are the CP-2 and CH-2 printed reports.

Public Use Microdata Files: The PUMs are computerized files containing a sample of individual long-form records showing most population and housing characteristics. Two PUMs are planned for 1990. The first is a 5 percent sample identifying county groups. The second is a 1 percent sample identifying MSAs used in the 1990 census.

These products are available directly from the Census Bureau—all on computer tape, some on CD-ROM—and the bureau distributes its CD-ROM products to federal depository libraries.

Current Population Survey (chapters 1, 2, and 8)

Each monthly CPS is the basis for a microdata file that presents information about the individuals within CPS sample households. These files appear several months after the survey is conducted and provide the basic labor force activity information that is collected each month, plus any additional data collected to supplement the basic survey.

Economic Censuses (chapter 2)

The results of the economic censuses (agriculture, construction, retail trade, wholesale trade, service industries, manufactures, mineral industries, and transportation) are disseminated in machine-readable form. The Census Bureau has traditionally provided access to this information on computer tape. Data from the economic censuses have also been released on CD-ROM, and the CD-ROMs are being provided to depository libraries.

Government Finance (chapter 7)

The data included in the GF series are released as the Survey of Governments, Annual Financial Statistics File, on computer tape. This survey is divided into three parts. File A provides state government financial data and a sample of local government data. File B provides aggregate local government data. File C provides national and state data by level and type of government.

Merchandise Imports and Exports (chapters 6 and 8)

Monthly tabulations on exports, imports, and shipping are available on computer tape and CD-ROM. These files are arranged differently and provide greater detail than their print counterparts. The CD-ROMs have been included in the federal depository program.

As of early 1991, Census Bureau data on computer tape were priced at $175 per reel. CD-ROMs were $125. To order products, contact Customer Services, Bureau of the Census, Washington, DC 20233.

U.S. Department of Agriculture

Farm Labor (chapters 2 and 8)

USDA statistical releases, including the results of the *Farm Labor* survey, are available in computerized form in the online service CIDS (Computerized Information Delivery Service). CIDS does not provide historical coverage; only the most current release is available online. For information on rates, contact Russell T. Forte in the Office of Public Affairs, USDA, Washington, DC 20250.

U.S. Office of Management and Budget

United States Budget (chapter 7)

The budget of the U.S. government is available from the National Technical Information Service (5285 Port Royal Road, Springfield, VA 22161) on computer tape. A variety of presentations is available as annual files for select years from 1966. A cumulative file, *Budget Data and Title Files (U.S. Government), 1940–1990*, is also available. This file contains fiscal year 1986 budget data files used to produce the printed *Historical Tables* and *Budget of the United States Government*. Data provided include budget authority, budget receipts, outlays, surpluses or deficits, and federal debt. Where necessary, data for years prior to 1986 have been restructured to be consistent with the 1986 budget. As of early 1991, the dataset was priced at $210.

Index

Jean Slemmons Stratford is head librarian, Institute of Governmental Affairs, University of California, Davis. She received her B.A. in English from the University of California, Berkeley, and her M.L.S. from the State University of New York at Albany. She has extensive experience with social and economic data, including machine-readable sources. Stratford has authored several articles in this field and co-authored a bibliography of statistical sources. She is a member of ALA's Government Documents Round Table and is active in the International Association for Social Science Information Service and Technology (IASSIST).

Juri Stratford is government documents librarian at the University of California, Davis. He received his B.A. in English from the University of California, Berkeley, and his M.L.S. from the State University of New York at Albany. He has extensive experience with social and economic data, including Census Bureau CD-ROMs. He has authored several articles in the field and co-authored a bibliography of statistical sources. Stratford is a member of ALA's Government Documents Round Table and is active in the IASSIST.